GUIDED BY THE SPIRIT

GUIDED BY THE SPIRIT
A Jesuit Perspective on Spiritual Direction

Frank J. Houdek, S.J.

Foreword by Howard J. Gray, S.J.

an imprint of
LOYOLA PRESS
Chicago

Loyola Press
3441 North Ashland Avenue
Chicago, Illinois 60657

New Testament quotes are the author's translations. Old Testament
quotes are from the Jerusalem Bible (London: Darton, Longman & Todd,
Ltd. and Doubleday and Co., 1968).

Cover design: Frederick Falkenberg
Interior design: Jill Mark Salyards
Cover photograph: Saint Ignatius writing the Constitutions. Portrait by
Jusepe de Ribera (ca. 1622), courtesy of Thomas Lucas, S.J.

Library of Congress Cataloging-in-Publication Data
Houdek, Francis Joseph.
    Guided by the Spirit: a Jesuit perspective on spiritual direction/Frank J.
    Houdek.
        p.   cm.
    Includes bibliographical references and index.
    ISBN 0-8294-0859-2 (alk. paper)
    1. Spiritual direction. 2. Spiritual directors. I. Title.
BX2350.7.H68 1995   95-8779
253.5'3--dc20   CIP

Contents

Foreword

One of the more attractive ministries of the early Jesuits was spiritual conversation, the art of sharing in easy familiarity how God is present in human experiences. While Ignatius Loyola and his companions had no exclusive purchase on this ministry, they did give it an honored place as another instance of revealing the Word of God. Frank Houdek's reflections on the art of spiritual direction are a contemporary realization of this tradition.

We look for wisdom and compassion in spiritual direction, the ability to help us see God at work even in areas of weakness and struggle. We want to feel that we have been heard with reverence and dealt with honestly. We want our freedom honored and our ambitions challenged. We want to know God's love as empowering our efforts to live the Christian life with humane integrity. In brief, we want an array of gifts only God can provide.

It is a tribute to Frank Houdek that he has kept all these desires in clear focus and responded to them with gentle clarity. Reading *Guided by the Spirit* is to enter into conversation with a master of contemporary Ignatian spirituality.

Howard J. Gray, S.J.
University of Detroit–Mercy

Acknowledgments

I thank all those directors and directees who have taught me about the ministry of spiritual direction. Without their gift *Guided by the Spirit* could not have been written. I learned so much from them about direction; it is their wisdom that appears in this book. Although it would be impossible or inappropriate to thank everyone by name, I am deeply grateful to all of them. I do wish, however, to single out a few in a special way.

The late David Asselin, S.J., taught me about the gift of spiritual direction. He directed me personally and supervised me during my earliest experiences of direction. I always will remain grateful for his care and his wisdom. I am also deeply grateful to Walter Farrell, S.J., for his personal care and mentoring and for his constant support over the past quarter of a century.

I cannot thank enough the students of the Jesuit School of Theology at Berkeley with whom I have shared this material. Their reactions and feedback have made this a far better book than it would have been without them. I am deeply grateful to Thomas Gleeson, S.J., president of the Jesuit School of Theology, for providing me with the time and leisure to complete this project. I thank Jean Blomquist, my editor, for her patient and competent work with what was an unruly manuscript. She tamed it, and it is a better product because of her.

Many people have given me personal support as I struggled with this project. I am forever in their debt. In particular, I thank John Murphy, S.J., and Robert Fabing, S.J., for their friendship and encouragement.

Finally, I am most grateful to Penny Pendola of the Diocese of Oakland. She was a constant support throughout.

I am especially thankful for all the ways that she helped bring *Guided by the Spirit* to completion.

Introduction

What is spiritual direction? What assumptions do I hold that affect my understanding and practice of spiritual direction? Before we begin our exploration of spiritual direction, I want to address these important questions. They provide the foundation and framework that undergird and shape my understanding and practice of spiritual direction.

My definition of and assumptions about spiritual direction grow out of my own experience and reflection. Though I now take them largely for granted, I have at one time or another examined, critiqued, and tested them for their authenticity in my life and work as a spiritual director. However, as is often the case with spiritual matters, I know that they are not open to rational demonstration or intellectual arguments. Yet, because they are in large measure my working principles, it is important that I share them with you before we proceed further.

Working Assumptions

Let me turn to my working assumptions about God and the person seeking spiritual direction. I assume that God exists and is benignly concerned about the individual human person. I also assume that God exercises a caring concern about the entire human family. For the purpose of this work, I assume that there is a personal God who is positively and actively concerned about the well-being of the individual, indeed, all humankind. I am convinced that it is only from such an assumption that one can reflect upon the experience of spiritual direction.

My second assumption, or working principle, concerns the knowability of God. It is not enough simply to assume that God exists. I assume that God is knowable, that is, that God reveals divine mystery and reality to the human family in a variety of ways—through creation, the prophetic word, human relationships, events of history, the Incarnation of God, and personal and communal moments of mysterious gifts and graces. The knowability of God is an important working assumption. On it rests the very possibility of spiritual direction as I understand it.

Third, I assume that God invites us into relationship with God and with one another. Such relationships, of course, assume much about the reality and action of God: that God wills familiarity with us, that God wills relationships and community among us, that God sustains and supports human relationships, that God is an integral partner in these relationships.

In addition to these minimal assumptions about God, I also presume certain qualities in the person who seeks spiritual direction, such as experience, reflection, and articulation. By experience I mean that the person has a sense, an awareness, a sensibility of mystery in his or her life. The individual appreciates the mysterious realities that permeate one's existence. A person realizes that these realities defy or transcend ordinary human ways of knowing, analyzing, or understanding. Their intelligibility demands other ways of knowing. To use a word common in the Ignatian/Jesuit tradition, one occasionally experiences *sentir,* a felt knowledge that one walks, lives, or experiences the self in a context of mystery. Often this intuition becomes the event or catalyst that provokes the person to seek spiritual direction.

I also assume that the person has a minimal capacity for self-reflection. In saying this, I want to distinguish self-reflection from negative introspection. Self-reflection involves the personal ability to stand outside oneself in order to honestly and integrally view one's life. In this process one may act reverently toward oneself and confront all of one's experience. Self-reflection requires a minimum of selectivity and a maximum of reverential care for oneself.

It is an edifying process and one in which positive self-awareness and self-building occurs. Light and dark, virtue and vice, grace and sin are all open to examination. This examination leads to a deeper, more honest, and more accepting sense of oneself. It becomes a personal wisdom that sustains the person.

Negative introspection, on the other hand, is a process that is self-erosive and self-punitive. One harbors a negative prejudice or bias toward oneself. In its worst form, the person removes all positive feedback. Most of us, of course, have inclinations of negative introspection, moments when we view ourselves with a very jaundiced eye, placing the worst possible interpretation on our motives and questioning even our most altruistic actions. The result is an eroded sense and acceptance of ourselves. Occasional moments of negative introspection notwithstanding, the directee should be capable of experiencing the more positive and edifying exercise of personal self-reflection.

Finally, I assume that people seeking spiritual direction have a modicum of verbal skills. Not only are they aware of the full range of individual experience through self-reflection but also they have sufficient communication skills to share and articulate this experience with other human beings. Obviously, problems and difficulties may occur. Since some aspect of the experience to be shared is essentially ineffable, no language or concept, image or symbol, word or gesture will ever be entirely adequate to communicate it. All the person can do is try to approximate the reality and the quality of the experience.

These operational assumptions, these working principles, underpin the possibility and reality of spiritual direction. I assume that there is a merciful, compassionate, and mysterious Other—God—who cares enough about us collectively and individually to communicate with the human family and the individual members of the human family. This God is knowable and manifests divine mystery in manifold ways, all aimed at drawing us more deeply into relationship with

God. I assume that a person who is seeking spiritual direction has experienced in some personal and unique fashion this mysterious Other. I also assume that the individual can reflect not only on this experience but also on the totality of life experiences and share these reflections in all their dimensions with others.

What Is Spiritual Direction?

Having described the assumptions that I believe make spiritual direction possible, I will now offer a descriptive definition of spiritual direction. To do so, let us look at two simple stories, one from secular literature, the other from the New Testament.

The first comes from George Bernard Shaw's play *St. Joan.* In a marvelous scene, Joan appears before the Inquisition. In the course of interrogation she reveals that much of her so-called questionable activity was determined by her desire to be responsive to voices that she had heard. The presiding judge interrupts and asks her, "Do you mean to tell us that you hear voices?" Joan pauses for a moment and replies, "Doesn't everyone?"

I invite you to pause here for a moment and reflect on Joan's question. Quietly consider the many and varied voices that you hear. When do they come? What do they mean? To which do you pay attention? Your answer to these simple questions reveals a great deal about the meaning and reality of spiritual direction. They allude to the sense of transcendence and mystery that pervades the life and experience of us all.

The second story, about two disciples on the road to Emmaus, occurs in the last chapter of the Gospel of Luke. Here are two human beings in the midst of a very troubling, confusing, and mysterious experience. They have suffered an incalculable loss—the violent death of a dearly beloved friend—but more than just a friend. Shocked and grieved, they fall into an incredibly deep depression. They do not understand what has happened. Despair envelops them, like the shadow of death. Rather than try to cope with their experience, they decide to flee in an attempt to diminish and control the pain and turmoil within them. They run away, just as we often do in response to painful and confusing experiences.

But then, in midst of their pain and grief, they are met on the road by a mysterious stranger. He joins them and engages them in serious conversation. Gradually, he questions them about their recent experience. The scriptural account does not elaborate on the fullness of their discussion, but it does intimate the conversational nature of the encounter. The stranger, Jesus, asks a simple question: "What is happening?" He provides an opportunity for them to share their experience, both the actual facts involved and their affective, cognitive, and behavioral responses. Moreover, he contextualizes the experience for them. That is, he places it in the context of revelation and their shared faith, beginning with Moses and the prophets, in the rich and varied ways that God always has revealed divine mystery to his people. A process of interpretation occurs. What was once ambiguous is now clear. Light is shed on the darkness; new meaning evolves from dialogue. The affective experience of these disciples is accepted without any harsh criticism or judgment; it is, in fact, tempered by a new emotional awareness and sensibility. The decision to flee is now seen as misguided. Because a new sense of mystery has unfolded, a new decision can be made for the well-being of the people involved and the entire believing community.

What happened? What bearing does this event have on the meaning of spiritual direction? Why have I introduced in some detail this Gospel narrative into a discussion about spiritual direction? Likewise, what does the story of Saint Joan, shared earlier, have to do with spiritual direction?

From these two stories we can draw a descriptive definition of spiritual direction. Spiritual direction is a conversation, a dialogue, between two people. In such a conversation one person aids another, often by a process of question and answer, to express his or her experience of personal faith and personal mystery. In this way one can discover the origin, the character, the quality and movement, and the patterns that evolve. One learns to hear more clearly and discriminate more acutely the varied voices of personal experience. This clarification, this discovery and interpretation, empowers the individual to make decisions that are congruent with and in greater harmony with a personal and unique experience of faith and mystery.

Three central elements are involved in this description of spiritual direction. First, it is a personal encounter that is conversational. It is not an account read to someone or a sharing of one's personal spiritual journal, nor is it a static report of what has transpired or a manuscript that someone reads. It is a true dialogue. Both parties in the conversation play a distinctive and necessary role. Real mutuality is important if the mysterious dimension of experience is to be discovered. All the life-experience of both parties—faith, commitment, talents and gifts, disappointments and failures—are at work in this dialogue, even though the development and growth of only one of the people, the directee, is prioritized.

Second, the primary purpose of the conversation is to express faith and mystery. It is an opportunity to clarify and to objectify, to come to grips with what is going on in our personal and subjective experience of the world, of God, of others, and of self. It is a needed, personal opportunity to appropriate our inner world of faith, mystery, and belief. Through this conversation we assimilate the reality of our interior life. We struggle to express, to conceptualize, to frame our experience in words, symbols, or images, even as we realize that this expression will never adequately fit the lived reality of the mystery as the person actually experienced it.

Spiritual direction, then, is the opportunity we offer ourselves to raise our deepest experience to conscious faith. It is the patient effort to recognize God's mysterious and loving presence with us in all levels of our being and experience. Words are our normal tool of communication, tools that have a way of challenging us to say what we actually mean. At its best, spiritual direction is one situation in which we cast aside false rhetoric and admit, with full honesty, the complete range of our lived experience.

Third, the secondary purpose of this dialogue is spiritual discretion or discernment—that is, the attempt to understand the origin, meaning, direction, and purpose of our experience and to make behavioral decisions that are congruent with this experience. If we pursue honest communication, we can better understand what is happening in our lives with God, and we can appreciate better where God is leading us. We find deeper meaning in the overall direction of our lives, in our moods and movements. We pick up some sense of the rhythm and pattern, of the dynamic of God's touch, of God's purchase on our lives, our hearts, and our spirits. We know what voices we hear, and we know what voices we respond to by the choices that we make before the living God.

We can also say what spiritual direction is not. Spiritual direction is not psychological counseling or psychotherapy. These two disciplines ordinarily concentrate on problem areas of life and generally seek resolution through an emotional understanding of personal history or by modifying personal decision making and behavior from a psychodynamic perspective. This interpersonal relationship may lack any conscious awareness or reference to God, mystery, or faith. In contrast, spiritual direction deals explicitly with spiritual themes in life, embracing the totality of one's life and experience.

Spiritual direction is not simply solving problems or making decisions. Although problem solving and decision making can occur during spiritual direction, they are not its primary purpose. Solving problems and making decisions necessitate receiving advice and generally emphasize one area of a person's life. Further, they are often restricted to a time of crisis. In contrast, spiritual direction is concerned about a person's life in all its dimensions and at every moment because God can reveal mystery at all times and in all experiences.

Finally, spiritual direction is not simply a matter of friends getting together to talk seriously about life. Friends are often afraid to say important or difficult things to one another. The desire to sustain a friendship can overcome the need to speak the truth. Hence, the Pauline injunction always to speak the truth in love—the centerpiece of spiritual direction—is violated.

It should now be clear that there is really only one objective in spiritual direction: the development or growth of the individual seeking spiritual direction, otherwise known as the directee. It is important to remember that the growth of the person is not determined in any prearranged fashion by the director or anyone other than the directee. Rather it is determined by the directee in prayer, in reflection, and in the relationship with the living God. The spiritual growth of the directee—in faith, hope, and love—is the explicit object, not a byproduct of spiritual direction. In the strictest sense, direction is a process of ongoing conversation initiated by the directee for the particular purpose of personal growth and development in the life of faith and mystery. The guide/director enters this dialogue only at the explicit invitation of the directee and only to facilitate such growth and development.

In short, spiritual direction is the work of the Spirit of God directing the individual human spirit in a Godward movement and direction. It is the Spirit of God acting with and within the human spirit in the living God. It is this mysterious attraction by and to God that occurs when one seeks spiritual direction. The role of the spiritual director is, at best, a collaborative one. The director collaborates with the person and with the Spirit of God to discover, evaluate, and encourage the very direction initiated by God's loving and ever-present Spirit.

I want to emphasize that spiritual direction is an *art*. As such, I do not believe that spiritual direction, in its fullest and most authentic sense, can be taught although it does utilize skills that can be learned. Even so, the gifts of grace, nature, temperament, and experience, which form the heart of spiritual direction, cannot be taught.

True spiritual directors do not call themselves to their work. They are empowered by a particular invitation from the community, from individuals who seek them out as companions and guides in their search for the living and loving God. Spiritual directors of true gift, skill, experience, and intuition know the ways of the human spirit, but only some of the ways of God's Spirit. They are at home in the world of God and thus are empowered to facilitate the faith quest and journey of others.

Thus, the person who directs "from the book" using only skills that can be learned will most likely be a poor director and of very little help. Worse, a poor director can be harmful to others. Therefore it is essential that those who desire to be spiritual directors prayerfully and carefully discern the true nature of their call and of their gifts and skills.

Current Interest in Direction

Before we examine spiritual direction, I wish to comment on the current and growing interest in direction. Why has literature on spiritual direction proliferated in recent years? To what palpable need does this literature respond? Why is interest in spiritual direction so great today?

In some ways the answers to these questions grow out of the Freudian revolution and its subsequent expressions. By the middle of the twentieth century, psychology and the related human sciences promised great hope for health, wholeness, efficiency, happiness, and enhanced personal relationships. Psychoanalysis and psychotherapy eclipsed spiritual direction and became the primary remedies for alleviating mental and emotional disorders. Therapists and clinicians, deemed to hold the key to the reality of psychological wholeness, became the new "clergy," the new "priesthood." Great trust was placed in the promise of therapy to end all human ills.

Unfortunately, the promise was not fulfilled. Psychoanalysis and psychotherapy lost their luster. Many people found them ineffective. Disenchantment with analysis, group work, and self-help regimens grew. Men and women, after undergoing various forms of therapy, still struggled to find meaning and purpose in their lives. Bernard Lonergan expressed this frustration when he wrote:

> In our lives there still comes the moment of existential crisis when we find out for ourselves that we have to decide for ourselves what we by our choices and decisions are to make of ourselves, but the psychologists and phenomenologists and existentialists have revealed to us our myriad potentialities without pointing out the tree of life, without unraveling the secret of good and evil. And when we turn from our mysterious interiority to the world about us for instruction, we are confronted with a similar multiplicity, an endless refinement, a great technical exactness, and an ultimate inconclusiveness. (Bernard Lonergan, "Dimensions of Meaning," in *Collection* [New York: Herder and Herder, 1967], 264.)

As people continued to seek the "tree of life," increasing numbers turned away from the realm of psychology and psychotherapy, turning instead to the world of religious phenomena. New movements and religious expressions arose in response, including the new evangelism and Pentecostalism, the charismatic renewal, and various Asian religions geared toward Western sensibilities and sensitivities.

Some turned (or returned) to Christian roots to seek sustenance. Interest in things spiritual and in spiritual direction itself grew. Many people sensed their deep need and desire for spiritual guidance, to have people of wisdom accompany them in their quest for meaning, purpose, value, and direction in their lives. Unfortunately, the Catholic Church and many other Christian denominations were ill-prepared since the number of qualified directors could not keep up with the demand.

As the need for spiritual direction became more apparent, many gifted directors turned their attention to training others. Old traditions of spirituality and spiritual direction were reclaimed; new schools of spiritual direction evolved. Spiritual directors began to incorporate new approaches into their work. The former authoritarian modes yielded to a more mutual style in which the director put his or her personal experience at the service of the directee. Shared prayer and increased contemplative awareness and attitudes became part of the spiritual direction experience. Forms of prayer other than discursive meditation were recognized and encouraged: centering prayer was rediscovered, and Jungian insights became an ordinary part of the spiritual direction dialogue. In addition, the ancient Christian ministry of healing was reinstituted. There was a return to a scriptural emphasis in prayer rather than on stylized or formalized books of spiritual reading or meditation. Concerns about social justice and institutional injustice became major issues of the personal spiritual journey. Further, the lived experience of women as directors and directees took on a new and major significance.

These important developments marked the years immediately following Vatican II and continued well into the 1970s. More recent religious and social developments have influenced contemporary spiritual direction as well: an intense social consciousness; the feminization of our culture (including its critique of myths, metaphors, enculturation patterns, and the use and abuse of authority); the experience of alienation and the concomitant yearning for intimacy; a deep disenchantment with consumerism; a rising consciousness of institutional injustice; a profound distrust of the military-industrial complex; growing anxiety about the threat of nuclear destruction; and the gradual dissolution of a formalized structure of religious duties, obligations, and practices that narrowly define "spiritual life."

Three basic forces underlie these developments: (1) a clear disenchantment with and distrust of conventional institutional religion and religious practice; (2) a deepened desire and heightened longing for transcendence, that is, new and deeper ways of experiencing the Divine, the numinous, and the mysterious; and (3) a growing practical concern for peace and justice, human liberation and fulfillment. For many people, these forces fuel their quest for a sense of personal authenticity that can be developed through a combination of personal prayer and reflection. These needs lead to a deep desire for a compassionate discerner as a companion in the quest for meaning, value, direction, and purpose. Spiritual direction then becomes an avenue for helping people to understand, integrate, and commit themselves to a life of encountering, engaging, and surrendering to the movements of the Divine.

What Follows?

Given this deep need and desire for the Divine and the subsequent seeking of spiritual guidance, let us now turn to a closer examination of spiritual direction itself. In the remainder of this book, we will look at various facets of a developed relationship with the God of mystery. Areas of specific focus include types of directees and their particular needs in direction, prayer and spiritual discernment, the relationship between director and directee (including its inner dynamics and pitfalls as well as its joys and graces), the qualities of the spiritual director, and the training and experience necessary for the ministry of spiritual direction.

My reflections evolve from my own experience of more than thirty years in spiritual direction as well as the gifts and experience of many others in the ministry. *Guided by the Spirit* is not a definitive work, yet I do believe that through research and reflection I have gained valuable knowledge of and insight into the reality and process of spiritual direction. In addition to doing individual spiritual direction, I have conducted or been part of numerous institutes and workshops on spiritual direction. I have also supervised many new directors. These activities have enriched my own life and work, and I am eager to share the fruit of these experiences with you.

Further Reading

William A. Barry, S.J., *Spiritual Direction and the Encounter with God: A Theological Inquiry* (Mahwah, N.J.: Paulist Press, 1992).

Thomas Hart, *The Art of Christian Listening* (Mahwah, N.J.: Paulist Press, 1980).

Sandra Schneiders, I.H.M., "The Contemporary Ministry of Spiritual Direction," *Chicago Studies* 15 (spring 1976): 119–35.

1

The Directee and the Process of Spiritual Growth

A few introductory remarks are necessary on the directee and the process of spiritual growth. No less than Saint Ignatius of Loyola offers a bit of practical wisdom: one can make no greater mistake or do no greater harm than to direct others as one directs him- or herself. Ignatius was warning us against missing the uniqueness of the person who is being directed. He wanted to make it clear that no two persons will ever profit from the same kind of direction, because God deals with each person uniquely, specifically, and appropriately. Thus, recognizing the subjective, personal, and unique reality of an individual will always be more important for the director than identifying recognizable types or predictable processes of spiritual growth. Obviously, the kind of person conducting the spiritual direction is also very important. The director must be open to the differences that exist between directees, yet free enough to risk entering the uniqueness of another person's personal experience.

Even so, a director must be aware of some of the "typical" patterns of growth and development in directees. This wisdom has passed from generation to generation of Christians and forms what we might call the classical ascetic tradition. Such a tradition has a variety of limitations that needs to be complemented by contemporary theological and psychological developments. Still this tradition provides a basic framework from which a director can witness the working of God's Spirit in the unique human being placed before him or her.

Some Preliminary Reflections on the Directee

Let us begin with some preliminary reflections and remarks about language usage. It is important to note that I will be using the language that has been generally accepted within spiritual direction, even though such terms as *director* and *directee* may have negative or authoritarian connotations for some readers. Already, attempts have been made to substitute alternate expressions; for example, a few may speak of a guide, a spiritual friend, or a soul friend or may call the directee a seeker, a pilgrim, or a journeyer. These alternatives have met with more than a little success. Although I find some of them attractive—and can understand their popular appeal—I have chosen to retain traditional terminology in the hope that my treatment will eliminate any negative implications.

I believe the only person who should seek spiritual direction is the person who can use it well, that is, someone who actually wants to grow and profit from direction. This person should experience a pressing need for direction, a felt need, and be willing to make a commitment and accept the demands that such a commitment entails.

The need for direction can be felt at certain turning points in one's life, such as a midlife crisis, notable changes in one's prayer or life situation, a new relationship that requires insight or illumination, new tasks that need to be done, or new expectations that are placed upon the person. It can arise from experiences of loss, failure, or separation. Any significant change of environment may provoke this sense of need. Whatever the situation, the person experiences a felt need to integrate and make sense of his or her life at a higher level of meaning.

It is important to reiterate the qualities that the directee is presumed to have at the beginning of a spiritual direction relationship: the directee has a sense or awareness of experience; the directee knows that something mysterious and compelling is about to happen; the directee possesses reflective skills, or what Swiss psychologist Jean Piaget calls "some species of formal operational thinking"; and the directee has the verbal skills to communicate significant lived experiences to the director.

During the first few meetings, as mutual trust and confidence grow, both the director and the directee need to make a provisional evaluation, a judgment about the feasibility or viability of the relationship and the chances that it will be productive for the directee and facilitate the directee's spiritual growth and development. Once mutual trust and confidence have been established, both parties should make a judgment about the viability of the relationship. They should make this evaluation as quickly as possible, for it is in the best interest of the directee to do so. Although spiritual direction is a mutually binding agreement, it does leave the directee with the freedom at any time to reevaluate the relationship and, if necessary, terminate it. In other words, ordinarily the director does not have the prerogative to end the relationship, unless it is clear that it is not serving the best interests of the directee. The director has freely placed his or her talent, experience, and insight at the service of the directee. For the director to withdraw arbitrarily from the relationship after the directee has become vulnerable is either unfair or destructive to the directee—or both.

What the director is seeking during these first few meetings is a broad openness and trust in the directee along with a strong desire for growth in awareness and responsiveness to the living God. It is on the basis of these attitudes or dispositions that the director and directee together can evaluate the possibilities inherent in the relationship.

A major part of the experience and skill of the director during these initial meetings is the ability to distinguish a directee with problems from one with a problem personality who is seeking in spiritual direction what should more aptly be sought in psychotherapy, psychological counseling, or another form of human assistance. For example, some people enter clinical pastoral education (CPE) for all the wrong reasons. They are seeking from a professional ministry training program the kind of self-awareness or alleviation of emotional distress that can only be found in professional therapy. Often their presence in a CPE group is nothing but personal avoidance of their problems and deeply destructive to the group. Similarly, individuals seek spiritual direction for purposes other than growth in faith and awareness of God. They seek spiritual direction as a substitute for clinical psychotherapy. It is the role of the director to recognize these problem personalities and refer them to the appropriate agencies. Any other decision by a director is more likely to be harmful to the directee. At best it aids and abets the directee in avoiding the very reality needed for healing, peace, emotional balance, and personal happiness.

This does not mean, of course, that those who are being helped by a therapist or professional counselor are incapable of entering spiritual direction. In fact, it is often possible for a therapist and spiritual director to work in tandem for the well-being of the same person. Though the focus and area of expertise of each may differ notably, both a spiritual director and a therapist can and often do collaborate in a process that is liberating for the directee. In such a case, I believe that the director should generally support the work and direction of the therapist.

A minimum of human compatibility between director and directee is essential for the establishment of an honest, open, and trusting relationship. The director needs to have some humility, including the ability to recognize personal limitations and to realize that one cannot be spiritual director to everyone. Certain people just cannot talk openly and honestly with one another; it cannot be helped. This realization must remain a point of honest and ongoing self-examination for even the best and most gifted of spiritual directors.

Patterns of Spiritual Growth and Development

Various ways exist to speak of growth or development of directees, as well as various ways to classify and typify directees. As we look at these approaches, let us begin with the classical ascetic tradition, which is rooted largely in the work and insight of Saint John of the Cross. I will use his descriptions and examples as indicators of the various types of directees and the stages of growth and development that are typical and appropriate to each type. I must emphasize that the work, role, and involvement of the director differs with each type of directee and at each stage of the directee's journey. Once again, it is of paramount importance to state the fundamental principle of spiritual direction. One can make no greater mistake as a director than to direct every directee in exactly the same way. To do so denies two fundamental realities: (1) it is God's Spirit that actually directs the person and (2) each person is unique before the living God.

Direction for Beginners

Beginners are only now starting their journey to a life of meaning, value, and purpose and to a life directed toward God. Let me elaborate a bit and state something of the inner dynamics of this process for the "beginner" directee. It is also important to know what a competent and knowledgeable director can do with such beginners.

What do beginners look like? How do they present themselves to a director? What kind of self-revelation do they offer? Beginners want to clarify the goal of their personal journey. They do not yet have a road map; they possess a rudimentary and primitive sense of direction, quite amorphous and unfocused at this stage of the journey. The director may begin by simply asking them what they yearn for, what they want, and why they seek spiritual direction. In some instinctive and inchoate fashion, beginners recognize that the goal of their journey is an intimacy with God that will affect the entirety of their lives. The spiritual direction conversation centers on the specific shape of *this* goal for *this* person: how is this person going to find an awareness of and responsiveness to God? The director introduces the person to the means of attaining this goal, means that are already part of the grace and gift and invitation of the living God: prayer, virtue, ordered relationship, self-awareness, self-examination, and deep and real self-appropriation. None of this occurs accidentally, neither the clarification of one's personal direction nor the personal assimilation of the actual gift of God the person. The director encourages and challenges the directee to understand that real growth in faith and awareness of God will not take place without prayer, without self-reflection, and without the practice of Christian virtue. The director is in a delicate position, because he or she must avoid supporting belief systems that maintain that individuals literally can save themselves. To accomplish this feat the director must possess a healthy balance of maturity and sophistication.

Frequently, beginners are confronted with a variety of disordered relationships in their lives. They often treat people as a means to an end or as objects to be manipulated for the satisfaction of their personal desires, such as career advancement, emotional security, self-esteem, sexual needs. They use and abuse people, often unconsciously, or, when they are aware, without embarrassment. The directee denies or rationalizes these relationships by exclaiming, "Everyone does it!" It is the responsibility of the director to uncover any destructive tendencies of the directee. Open and honest charity must replace manipulation and oppression. The director must recommend, support, and encourage this kind of behavior.

During this early stage in the process it is best to remember that the directee sought spiritual direction because of a yearning or desire for meaning and value in life. This yearning helps the directee to persevere during times when the director may challenge, provoke, or make difficult demands.

Beginners emphasize affections of the heart—feelings, images, and desires—or whatever will provide emotional satisfaction. The pleasure/pain principle is often at work, so that the person focuses on whatever maximizes personal pleasure and avoids whatever provokes discomfort or pain. Recentering or refocusing the affections on God or values—that is, the very yearnings that led the person to begin spiritual direction in the first place—becomes crucial. Directees need both to be challenged and encouraged so that the deep desires that they have for God can be nurtured. This nurturing can be done through prayer, self-reflection, and a renewed personal relationship that allows charity to develop and flourish. Difficult though it may be, both director and directee need to be mutually committed to offering intercessory prayer for each other.

Beginners already have been truly converted to God; they have a sense of conversion, a movement away from a better place of mystery and value. They have brief, recurring episodes of meaning in which they actually experience the goal of their journey. They are very sincere about their desire for God but are not sure how to relate to God, the self, the world, and other human beings. At this point in their pilgrimage they are driven by a desire for personal gratification in every dimension of life, including religious activity. They want God to act as a spiritual equivalent of the sensual satisfaction that has been heretofore the focus of their life. They are enmeshed in a kind of spiritual narcissism, from which it is very difficult to escape. As with other human beings, they wish to make God an object, a means to satisfy their own sensual desires. In other words, God becomes just another being who is obliged to give them satisfaction and pleasure.

But this is not who God is or how the Spirit of God works. God desires the well-being and growth of each person, the development of freedom, responsibility, and the capacity for love and maturity. For this to happen, a reordering must occur. Directees must shift their focus to something other than sensual satisfaction or the pleasure/pain principle that previously guided their life choices.

Because the Spirit of God invites people in a wholly other direction, beginning directees experience a resistance to God's direction and the activity of God's Spirit. They deny, rationalize ("this is really okay"), or intellectualize ("there is really nothing wrong with manipulating people, because I deserve to succeed" or "everyone does this sort of thing"). Conflicting desires provoke strong feelings of emotional distress. The desire for God—which is deep, real, and compelling—clashes with the pattern of experiences, attitudes, and actions that will not lead the person to God. Numerous interior conflicts are accompanied by feelings of anxiety, confusion, fear, dread, and, sometimes, even rage at God, the spiritual director, or both. The director must pray for the wisdom and courage to negotiate stressful situations successfully for the well-being of the directee.

Once this conflicting interior reality is revealed through prayer, self-reflection, and spiritual direction, the directee tends to become angry, hostile, dependent, and unwilling to assume personal responsibility. The directee also becomes manipulative or unconsciously dishonest with self, God, and the director. Feeling threatened, the directee resorts to any and every means to maintain the disordered and self-defeating defenses of the psyche.

At this point the directee may become preoccupied with the director in a manner that has a real but covert sexual component to it. This sexual fascination with the director can be very flattering but also disruptive of the direction relationship and generally erosive of the well-being of the directee, especially if the director allows the fascination to grow and be acted out.

What can the director do for the directee at this time? Asking the directee to keep a journal can be very helpful. Journaling encourages more immediate awareness of and access to the interior turmoil experienced by the directee. This journaling revolves around experiences in both prayer and life, work and relationships, leisure and recreation, dreams and hopes. It should be a detailed journal that records important events and experiences, particularly the quality and direction of personal relationships.

Beginners will generally balk at journaling or any kind of self-reflection that focuses on their personal areas of resistance. They underplay or misstate their resistance to avoid conversing about it. They cannot allow to enter into consciousness anything that threatens them. They will include a "laundry list" of topics with their director, which will merely serve to avoid discussing their confusion, anger, fear, anxiety, or turmoil. In such cases, the director must become adept at understanding what is not being said or communicated. When ordinary human realities that form a typical part of everyone's life—such as family, work, fears, community, relationships, prayer, leisure, desires, yearnings, dreams—are consistently avoided by the directee, the director should be aware of this fact and, at some point, gently bring it to the directee's attention.

Beginners are often blind to their disorders. In fact, they are blind to their very blindness as well as to their strong and deep resistances. The director must gently help them be alert to their interior experience, to make it their own, and, where necessary, to order it. The operative questions are, "What do I need or want more than God?" and "What can I do about these needs with the help of God, so that God can become more central in my life and experience?" This gentle confrontation and collaboration between the director and directee will gradually prepare the person for the dark night of the senses in which God will communicate more directly.

In general, the type of prayer that most beginners choose is meditation. To be more precise, it is discursive prayer in which reasoning and thinking play a major role. The person aggressively thinks, imagines, and even desires. The object of this kind of prayer is to obtain personal truth, that is, the reality and truth of one's own life. The person realizes how things really are and how things could or should be.

Direction for Directees Being Purified by God

The first indication that significant interior ordering has occurred is the move away from meditation to contemplation as the dominant style or form of prayer. What is the shape of this movement? How is it seen and discerned by the director? How is it experienced by the directee? How is this gift of prayer distinguished from the kind of prayer typical of beginners? Contemplative prayer is much more passive than the meditative style of prayer; the directee becomes the patient rather than the agent and realizes that something is happening or something is being done to him or her. The directee is passive in prayer, not active. Thus, prayer loses much of its discursive quality; there is less thinking, less analysis, less reasoning, less seeking for personal truth and more intuitiveness, more imagination, and more emotion. God is not only more present but also more mysterious. God projects an Other quality. This web of interior realities marks the next stage of spiritual development. God is now revealed as startlingly more transcendent and increasingly more extraordinary.

The passage from meditation to contemplation signals a transformation of motivation and intention. Sensual satisfaction and a notable preoccupation with self are no longer the primary motivations. They are replaced by a deeper and active love of God, of self, and of neighbor. Occasionally, too, a real desire emerges to extend oneself for the well-being of one's neighbor, a realization that one's life is not only one's own but also that it is held in trust to others. Self-transcendence becomes a value and a real possibility. Disorder, imperfection, even intentional sin are replaced with true and active virtue as well as a better sense of love for oneself, a habitual caring for others, and a moderation of irrational or excessive fear or anger. The directee's new sense of self is attractive and energizing, forming a healthy and holy direction for personal growth and development. The person now actively realizes that God's intention is indeed directed toward personal freedom, personal responsibility, and personal maturity.

God's presence, action, and love are experienced more deeply within the person and within the larger dimension of life—in work, in relationships, in prayer, and in leisure. This strengthening presence has a deeper interior effect, for it produces extremely intense "dryness" in the person. Three qualities characterize this dryness: (1) a loss of personal consolation or "joying" in God or the creation of God. The person does not "enjoy" these realities any longer; (2) a new conscious, intense, and painful desire for God. The desire for God that began the process of growth and development is now intensified in a manner that causes much personal anguish and distress; and (3) an increasing inability to do meditation or be discursive in personal prayer. The old ways of active, cognitive prayer no longer work. The interior landscape has shifted, and the person cannot pray in the ways that were appropriate for the beginner.

This shift in prayer is an extremely important development for the directee. It is also a rather delicate situation that requires an element of sophistication from the director. A director may become anxious or fearful and consider the directee's new attitude a problem rather than a sign of maturity initiated by the Spirit of God. For this reason, the director must be especially alert and attentive.

It is not uncommon for inexperienced directors to become counterproductive at this point. Because they do not understand what is happening to the directee, they feel a need to rescue the person, to fix things up, and thus to make the directee feel better. They try many ways to alleviate the anxiety, confusion, or distress that the directee is feeling. This "savior complex" serves the needs of the director rather than the well-being of the directee. For the director to yield to this kind of temptation is wholly misguided.

What then can a competent director do when the directee is led by the Spirit of God in this time of dry darkness, this purifying activity of the living God? First, it is important for both the directee and the director to examine the cause of the phenomena in order to determine whether it is actually God's work or the result of poor response to grace on the part of the directee. Here the director needs to adopt a sophisticated approach in spiritual discernment, for there are two "states of soul" that, although they may appear similar, are quite different.

These two states have traditionally been described as *vagueness* and *obscurity*. Their superficial similarities can be very deceiving and have betrayed the competence of many spiritual directors who do not know how to discern the significant differences. In both cases the person can experience a significant attraction to prayer and to an increasing awareness of and familiarity with God. The person acts on this attraction and engages in personal prayer. Both times there is a sense that nothing is happening in prayer, that there is an emotional dryness. But significant differences do exist.

With vagueness, the experience is marked by an increasing temptation by the directee to provoke activity in prayer that is artificial or contrived. The person wants "to do something, to make something happen." Since there is no satisfaction in prayer, the person finds it increasingly tedious, demanding, and unrewarding. Finally, prayer is abandoned.

This vagueness describes the experience of someone who is being called by God to reform his or her behavior. An attachment or disordered behavior lies at the edge of consciousness, which the person knows intuitively. Although aware that the path does not lead to God, the person is nevertheless reluctant to let go. The Spirit of God continues to attract even though the person may, at the moment, prefer the dark side. Metaphorically speaking, God is inviting the person to do a waltz, but the person insists on doing the tango! For this reason, the person experiences discomfort in the presence of God despite a strong underlying attraction to prayer.

The disordered behavior or misguided attachment must be brought to consciousness and resolved before one can find peace in the presence of God in prayer. It is a question of discovering the truth about oneself, about one's behavior, about one's disposition, about one's living relationship with God. Meditation is the form of prayer that exposes one to such truth; self-reflection and Spirit-guided self-examination provide avenues of enlightenment and insight. The director must insist on this kind of prayerful activity if the vagueness is to be lifted and the directee is to begin growthful development once again.

Obscurity is an entirely different matter. It is the experience of one who is authentically seeking God and for whom the Spirit of God is leading through the dark night of the senses. Like vagueness there is a longing and a desire for prayer—to know the reality of God's presence in the gift of prayer. While consistently faithful in acting on this desire, the directee often describes prayer using such phrases as "nothing is happening" or "nothing is going on." There is affective and emotional aridity, a kind of experiential emptiness, little intellectual or imaginative activity, and a longing and desire for the action of God.

So far obscurity seems similar to the experience of vagueness. Here, however, the similarity ends. The directee does not experience any inclination or temptation to discontinue prayer. There is no desire to do busywork in prayer to facilitate affective, imaginative, or cognitive activity. Nothing contrived or artificial has a place in this experience. The person is determined to continue, to persevere in prayer, even though little or nothing is happening to convince the person that God is indeed active and present. However, an intuitive sense emerges that says it is good to be in prayer and that, though prayer may appear to be a waste of time, there is no better way to "waste" one's time than in the presence of the living God. Although directees may experience profound aridity in prayer, they are clearly aware that God is communicating divine mystery in the emptiness that now constitutes prayer. This Spirit of God actually teaches the person to be still and learn that God is indeed God—that God comes and goes as God chooses and that one must learn to be patient and wait to appreciate and savor the loving presence and action of God.

A director who lacks the sensitivity of understanding these apparently similar but essentially different realities will probably make some very bad mistakes. For example, the director may encourage the directee to be active and discursive in prayer, even though the Spirit is leading the directee to more nondiscursive and passive gifts of prayer. By encouraging such activity, the director is actually impeding the action of God's Spirit.

It is, therefore, important for the director to be knowledgeable and alert to the differences between vagueness and obscurity. Also it is imperative for the well-being and growth of the directee that the director make the critical discernment about the directee's state of soul. If this is not done carefully and accurately by the director, ill-prepared directees will be passive when they need to rely on meditative prayer. At the same time, those invited by God to be passive will probably be encouraged to pursue painful and regressive kinds of active and discursive prayer.

A director can and should help people who are experiencing obscurity in other ways. Certainly it is important to convey a sympathetic understanding of what is happening to the directees. Without such support, they may begin to think that something is dreadfully wrong, that they are doing or allowing something to distance them from the God whom they are seeking. Because of a sense of lost consolation, they will be inclined to return to prayers that are detrimental to their current growth and development.

It is important for the director to support the directee through this very difficult time and to help the directee to simplify prayer as much as possible. A director can share with the directee any helpful prayer techniques, such as centering prayer, breathing prayer, or using repetition as a way to focus consciousness in prayer. But the director must be careful. In no way should the director lead the directee to think or believe that these methods of prayer can control or constrict God. God will continue to come and go, to console or allow dryness, to be clearly present or seem absent. The point of sharing these styles of prayer is to support the work of the Spirit of God, to aid in simplifying prayer, and to help the person learn greater passivity to the action of God in life and prayer.

There is really no way to estimate how long this purifying activity of the Spirit will last. All one can say is it will remain as long as it is needed. Only God can read the heart and spirit of the directee and only God can really know what is needed by a person in the quest for God. This process ends when God chooses and when, in God's love and wisdom, the work of purification is accomplished.

Are there any signs to indicate that the work has been accomplished by the Spirit of God? Is there anything to indicate to the director that the purifying activity of God has been completed? Fortunately there are such indicators, and it is to these signs that a director should attend even while continuing to support the directee with sympathetic care, presence, and understanding. What then does the director seek to signal the end of this period of passive purification?

Direction for Directees Who Are "Proficient"

One indication that the period of passive purification has ended is when the person experiences or senses that growth has occurred. With increasing clarity directees realize that they are beckoned, invited, and called to experience the numinous and the mysterious. A reverence for the mystery of life and person increases. Though there may not be a greater intellectual clarity about God, there is a deeper assent to the reality of God in life and experience. Longing for God remains, but now this very longing is revelatory because the shape and intensity of the longing indicates what or who will fulfill it.

Directees realize that they are indeed moving in and to God and that the God-directed process of purification has been completed. A new and abiding serenity surfaces. The person is freer, liberated by the action of the Spirit of God. A desire to place life, energy, and talent at the service of God and neighbor has replaced disorder. Instead of discomfort or dryness in prayer, there are unexpected and episodic times of real joy, deep spiritual delight, and consolation in prayer.

Now is the time for the director to encourage active faith and sensitive charity—faith and charity that become incarnate in deeds and virtuous behavior. For it is clear that if there is no movement toward charity and concern for one's neighbor, then serious regression is possible. The directee must gradually surrender the old images of God, of idolatry, of limited concepts, of previous and perhaps consoling experiences of God.

Further, the directee must grow in the experiential understanding and realization that "fuzzy feelings" about God are not God. The affections that were once translucent and that allowed the light, warmth, presence, and love of God to shine are now opaque and can easily hinder the presence and action of God.

A new interior atmosphere of trust and personal freedom is developing. The director should note in the directee a greater personal recollection and interiority. There should be less need for devotional centering since the person is now able to find a much easier and much more immediate entry into prayer. Even when the spiritual joy of prayer is only episodic, a greater awareness of God's loving presence in many other dimensions of life can emerge. Though prayer may continue to be arid or dry, God provides a compensatory experience of divine presence in the fabric of life, particularly in personal relationships.

The director must be even more discerning, for it is still necessary to clarify the meaning of the experience with the directee. But there is a crucial difference, because the process of clarification is much more of a collaborative venture;

it is done in consort with the directee. In fact, the directee takes the lead in this new process of spiritual discernment. God's action and direction create a strong appreciation of the invitations of God and an eager and generous desire to be adequately responsive. Therefore, the director must collaborate with the directee in this process of clarification and assimilation. But, once again, the director must proceed wisely and cautiously. The act of discernment should not consist of any kind of pre-packaged solution to a problem. Rather the director should confirm the insight, illumination, and intuition of the directee and accept them as authentic clarifications of a very specific and unique personal experience. Only then will the directee's burgeoning powers of spiritual discernment, which are so important for further growth and development, be validated.

One cannot predict how long this state of soul will last. In fact, some people spend a good part of their adult spiritual life at this juncture. There are many reasons why this is so. Sometimes it is due to inept or incompetent spiritual direction! Sometimes the person's less than conscious (but very real) resistance to initiatives or challenges from God prevents further growth. Whatever the reason, many people do not continue the spiritual journey to deeper union with the living God.

What are the signs of transition to a deeper and different relationship with God? How are the director and directee to know that the Spirit of God is indeed taking new initiatives with the person? What are the realities that indicate movement, development, and growth into an unknown land where the landscape is very unfamiliar and can even be frightening? Finally, when the landscape is recognized, what can be done to continue the personal pilgrimage into this new spiritual terrain?

Direction for Directees
Who Are Being Further Purified by God

A time of final purification in which the living God is present awaits the person. In the earlier stage of personal purification much depended on the active work of the directee. During this final purification stage, however, the person remains wholly passive before the purifying action and presence of God. God completely takes over the process of purification in an all-encompassing manner. The entire project is strictly in the hands of God's Spirit.

In a very real sense this dark night of the spirit can be terrifying. It is characterized by an experience of light and wisdom. God communicates to the person with increased intensity. Intuitional awareness of God becomes stronger for the directee. There is a heightened or deepened experience of "knowing things I never knew I knew—about myself, my world, and my God!" There is an abundance of light, but it is the kind of light that is often purgative and painful. Earlier, the directee had discovered by grace a variety of disordered behaviors. Later, the directee learned the deeper personality traits in which the disordered behavior was rooted. In this final stage of purification, the person experiences great pain, a kind of personal embarrassment and humiliation. It is no longer a question of behavior, but of identity. The reality of God, his distance and sense of being different from us, comes as a revelation. The person acknowledges the ignorance of humankind and knows that God is wholly wise. The person is impotent against the profound power and majesty of God.

Yet this purging and purifying activity is not destructive in any way. It does not weaken or debilitate the person or cause depression. It does not erode the lived sense of personal goodness and gifts that marked the earlier stages of growth and development. God's wisdom illuminates and purifies the directee. The result is a deeper and more holistic centering of the person on God. Personal self-esteem, self-love, and self-reverence are not lessened or compromised. A new and profound realization of the truth, of goodness, and of the value of oneself before the living God emerges, along with a new sense of the mysterious power and grandeur of God.

Periods of anguish and spiritual delight alternate. Directees may experience distance from God, a deep sadness because they feel they are not worthy of God's love. Yet moments of great spiritual joy also can occur as the directee is purified and realizes more deeply the loving presence of God. These alternations of anguish and delight may confuse or trouble the directee, since they happen so intensely and so unexpectedly. But even this confusion or anxiety is not destructive or erosive.

Prior to this experience, the directee has done everything possible to cooperate and collaborate with the initiating gifts of the Spirit of God. Much remains to be accomplished by God to prepare the person to receive God's love and presence. Only God can work this amazing transformation. God must intervene in order for it to happen—to illumine and prepare and make the person ready for the further gifts of intimacy and familiarity. However, personal fear and resistance often prevent this precious gift from taking place.

What can the director do for the directee during this dark and difficult time? In what ways can the director facilitate the work of the Spirit of God in the directee? What should the director avoid? The best thing that a competent director can do during this time is to offer encouragement. So demanding and trying is this period for the directee that many are tempted to give up. Above all, the director must be a supporting presence for the directee. Once again it is necessary to clarify the meaning of the experience, that is, to assure the directee that this action of God is not to be questioned, avoided, or resisted. In short, the director encourages the person to have perseverance, hope, and courage. Often the very encouragement of the director empowers the directee to remain open to God's Spirit.

It is important that the director avoid any hint of "teaching." Of course, it is helpful for the directee to understand the nature of God's purifying activity. The director, however, should explain what is happening only to the extent that it helps the directee and avoid burdening the directee with any cognitive or intellectual views. To do so would be harmful if it becomes a way to escape from either prayer or from what God is actually affecting in the person. Any explanation that the director offers should communicate to the directee that this experience is a wonderful gift from God.

The director must continue to be very discerning and sensitive to the strength of the directee. Though God will not test the person beyond individual capacities, still there may be some need for time and space to re-gather one's strength, energy, and enthusiasm and allow the Spirit of God to further integrate, purify, and illuminate. A person may have to temporarily retreat from the intensity of the experience for a brief respite. The director should clearly state that this retreat is not to escape from God. Rather it is an opportunity to re-build one's energy and enthusiasm in order to be able to face and accommodate God.

In addition to encouragement and clarification, the director must be compassionate. In other words, the director must be available and offer honest and loving support to the directee. The director must spend additional time in prayer with and for the directee. The director must be strong when the directee feels unable to continue. The director does not take responsibility for the directee's life before God. Rather the director places personal resources at the discretion of the directee. During this difficult time of pilgrimage to God, the director may allow the directee to lean on or become temporarily dependent on him or her.

The only "sin" that a director can commit is to try to save a directee—that is, to usurp the liberating and saving action of God. Unfortunately, some (perhaps many) directors need peace, consolation, and absence of turmoil in their directees to confirm their own competence and ability and to bolster their own self-esteem. When one of their directees is in pain, they often make strenuous efforts to save the person—to alleviate the pain, assuage the discomfort, or rationalize the disarray. Such effort not only harms the directee but also disrupts the action of God in the directee.

Very often a director will aggressively encourage the directee to return to active modes of discursive prayer at a time when the Spirit of God leads in the direction of more passive and nondiscursive ways of prayer. In a sense the director sends the directee back to worship those very idols (images, feelings, concepts, symbols of God) that the Spirit of God is laboring to break down in the person. Fortunately, God loves the directee enough to overcome the ignorance or neediness of the director. Yet, purification may be unduly delayed because of the incompetence of the spiritual director.

Active purification cannot be hurried, for the process is wholly at the discretion of the living God. Though it can be prolonged by poor direction, it cannot be curtailed. God organizes both the conscious and unconscious dimensions of each personality. Often much time is needed for this process to mature and come to spiritual fruition.

Direction of Directees Who Have Been Purified

How then does one know when purification is completed? Purification is over when one is blessed and graced with a habitual, peaceful, joyous awareness and realization of God's love and presence in all the dimensions of life and activity. This awareness is no longer episodic or sporadic. It exists in conscious experience. The directee not only has a cognitive or intellectual realization of God's presence as a kind of abstract truth but also experiences a real awareness of joy, of peace, of truth about oneself and the mysterious reality of God. The experience withstands even when the stimuli of life would ordinarily and predictably provoke turmoil or confusion.

Saint Ignatius of Loyola epitomized this experience when he stopped to realize the loving presence of God in his life. In this way, too, the directee gradually realizes experientially that God is certainly, surely, and graciously the guiding force. No argument, debate, or discussion is necessary since there exists a certainty that is very convincing to both the director and the directee. It is up to the director to acknowledge this gift—to affirm it and rejoice in it with the directee.

From this point forward the person will need very little spiritual direction, for, in essence, the Holy Spirit has become the director. However, one notable pitfall still remains, one against which the director must struggle and labor to protect the directee: the very real danger of spiritual pride. Above all, the director must help the directee to avoid this insidious temptation. It is subtle and devious, because the person begins to feel invincible: "This is where I am; I have done all the right things. I have most adequately and very generously responded to God, and now God owes me this gift." Sometimes without even realizing it, the directee attributes the gift of God to individual effort, generosity, or cooperation with the earlier gifts of God. The director must help the directee to be aware of and avoid these feelings. When directing a person who has been gifted by God, the director must keep this issue in the forefront of the directee's consciousness.

Other than to affirm and help the directee avoid such pride, there is little else that a director can do with or for a person who has been gifted and graced by the loving action and presence of God. It is, of course, appropriate and helpful for both the directee and director to celebrate the gift together from time to time through shared prayer, eucharistic thanksgiving, and other such activities. Celebration and thanksgiving keep both aware of the giftedness of the situation. It is really the best defense against spiritual pride.

The director should remember one more thing. A style of spiritual hysteria exists that can resemble the final stage of spiritual growth and development of union with God. By this time, a directee will have read much pious, ascetical, and devotional literature, or hagiography, especially those of a traditional or sentimental nature. Such a person may appear rather esoteric—gifted with the kind of prayer life that one finds in books about prayer or the saints—and try aggressively to protect this false image. The directee will not allow the director to examine or probe the experience of life, prayer, or interpersonal relationships. Often the person uses the technical language of traditional ascetical theology to describe prayer. Thus, the directee implies that he or she possesses the gift of acquired contemplation and can be quite firm (though misguided) in this self-diagnosis.

In such a case it is important for the director to look at the person's quality of life, the person's history, and the quality of the person's relationships with God and others. It is also helpful to explore gently with the directee areas of fear, anger, and unresolved personal tensions. The presence and quality of these realities will determine either that the directee is indeed in a true experiential union with God or that neurotic spiritual hysteria is present.

The directee who is authentically led by the Spirit of God exhibits significant humility and a kind of "why me?" wonder at God's marvelous and gracious goodness. If such is the case, the director should be profoundly docile since there would clearly be no need for a spiritual director no matter how competent one may be.

These various stages of faith, growth, and development form a general and, perhaps, theoretical outline of the classical patterns of spiritual development. Each stage has clear characteristics and distinguishing signs; each has an appropriate and differing set of criteria for discernment. Each gives the director clues as to how to be present to the directee and how to facilitate the very development that has been initiated by the Spirit of God. Though based on the inherited tradition of the Christian community, these stages have indeed been confirmed by my own personal experience as a spiritual director. I have found this general classical pattern to be very much a part of the individuated experience of most of the people I have directed. My experience as a director tells me that this is not simply a theory that has no relationship to the lives of real people. Nor is it a theoretical construct laid upon the experiences of others that fails to understand the deepest realities. These things happen to real people. Understanding these patterns of spiritual growth and development has been of immense help to me as I have walked with countless others along their spiritual pilgrimage.

Further Elaboration of the Growth Pattern

Now I would like to elaborate further on this presentation, to flesh it out, as it were, from my own practical and lived experience of spiritual direction. As I describe this pattern of development in more detail, I will offer some practical aids and reflections for other directors who accompany their directees on life's difficult journey to God.

Probably the directees with the most tasks to accomplish and the most issues to resolve is the group that I have styled beginners. Four elements need to be resolved before they can experience further growth or development in God: (1) the processes of attention and awareness; (2) personal appropriation of the work of God; (3) commitment to the gifts of God and the process of personal growth; and (4) personal integration of God's action. A director should gently, constantly, and consciously attend to a few simple things. Although they are listed in chronological order, they frequently occur simultaneously; therefore, the director must be aware of them at all times.

First, the director should help directees to articulate, communicate, and be aware of their lived experience. The important question is simply, "What is happening currently in your life?" This question should be in the forefront of consciousness for both the director and the beginning directee. The spiritual direction dialogue should consistently concentrate on what is actually happening rather than turning to interpretation or evaluation too quickly. Often beginners are insensitive to their experience and do not turn to the important details that are revelatory of themselves and of God.

Second, the director and the directee should enter into a collaborative understanding and evaluation of the effect, images, feelings, and interpretations of the experience. Once directees are adequately aware of the depth and richness, the mystery and challenge of their experience, then the director should join them in exploring the fears, joys, and understanding that emerges. It is very important that the director know how to listen to the nonverbal communication of the directee, particularly the body language and the language of symbol, desire, dreams, and imagery. Often the director and the directee will need to work together to create a new language that the directee can use comfortably as a means of communication.

Third, the director must support the directee in an enabling and empowering fashion as the directee struggles for personal commitment—a commitment that emerges from the meaning, pattern, origin, and feelings of life, mystery, and God. The commitment should fit the person and provide empowerment for the future. This is the subtle stage in the direction of beginners. Up until now the process of growth and development has been "fun," because it has not made any notable demands on the directee. Because commitment is required now, the directee will likely resist the process of direction. It is important for the director to balance encouragement with accepting the challenge that offering spiritual direction evokes.

Finally, the director assists the person to develop options for concrete and authentic faith choices that will embody deep personal commitment. This personal commitment evolves from the directee's question, "What must I do to make real—in my flesh and bones and blood and spirit—my personal response to the real initiative of God that I have experienced?" The director supports the directee in a gentle and nondirective fashion to choose from among the options available for a personal faith response. Throughout the process the director also helps to evaluate the choices that the directee makes.

These ongoing tasks reflect the primary function of a beginning directee's work: awareness, personal appropriation, commitment, and conscious integration of experience. Let's take a closer look at these tasks and their relation to the spiritual development of the beginner. As we do, we will consider the following questions: What are the developmental tasks of a directee? What must a directee resolve when beckoned to the paths of faith, development, and growth? How do directees describe their experience as they take their first faltering steps on their journey of faith?

Attention and Awareness

Generally, God challenges beginners with a new awakening to spiritual reality. More than just awareness of or rational assent to theological truth, this reality is very personal and accompanied by deep feelings of joy or consolation, fear or agitation. New awarenesses arise from personal encounters, from reading, from beauty in nature, from worship that deeply touches the person, from times of conflict or personal crisis. The truth or presence of mysterious reality is clear and demanding. Faith, Spirit, mystery, or love deeply touch and move the person. The directee realizes that God can be taken seriously. The personal question now becomes, "What do I do with all of this?"

It is especially crucial that the director facilitate the process of awareness and articulation. Often the experience of mystery has an apparent simplicity about it, but it is loaded with meaning and subjective connotations that are working transformations in the spirit and psyche of the person. These connotations have to be expressed and externalized so that the full richness and complexity of the experience can be understood and appreciated by the directee. The beginner holds a deep-seated need to savor the experience(s) that provoked this new awareness of God. Often there will be faltering attempts to recreate the experience through memory. It is like Paul recounting his own experience of personal conversion. Each account in the Acts of the Apostles is richer, more embellished, and more supportive of his commitment to be Christ's apostle.

Personal Appropriation

The struggle to be aware and search the depths of this new experience begins the inner process of personal appropriation—making one's own the events that have provoked an awareness of the mysterious dimension of life. Clarifying and searching for the inner meaning of the experience makes it part of the history and personality of the directee. Facts are reflected upon, implications are explored, patterns of meaning are discovered, deep affections are enjoyed, and courage for commitment is evoked. Here the person meets the Spirit of God with reverence and reflective seriousness.

The appropriate type of prayer to use is the prayer of meditation, that is, a discursive prayer whose object is personal truth—the truth of one's self, one's world, and one's relationships with God and the people who inhabit one's world.

Faith now becomes more than mere concepts or ideas. The need for a new posture toward life emerges. The directee realizes the importance of the journey that is about to begin but does not know where the path will lead. The beginner faces the difficult challenge of leaving the security of the known world for the unknown. It is a time to accept a challenging personal commitment. It is to this commitment that both the director and directee must turn their shared attention.

The challenge is very real. A directee may experience considerable vacillation and a good deal of anxiety. Anxiety can have various causes. The clarity and certitude that most people crave is gone. They can be faint-hearted and lack the necessary courage to face the implications of this call to personal commitment. They may realize that they will never again belong to self in the same old way, because they belong wholly to God in a new way. They shrink from surrender to the Spirit of God. All of these factors provoke significant anxiety.

Commitment to the Gifts of God

In addition, the directee undergoes an interior ambivalence or ambiguity. On the one hand, directees may exhibit a strong inclination and attraction to respond to the challenge of commitment. Fervor, enthusiasm, and affective intensity are all intimately associated with conversion and commitment. Largeness of heart and magnanimity are at work: the directee really wants to be generous. On the other hand, largely unconscious forces also play their part: fear, resistance, and self-protectiveness. Other factors include laziness, inertia, and, sometimes, paralysis.

The real challenge is to adjust one's life to this new commitment. Values, needs, relationships, and work have to be adjusted radically to conform to the quality of the conversion experience. The beginner is challenged to make life more intentional, less lived by chance or happenstance. Critical reflection, which is needed in every dimension of life, replaces unreflective spontaneity. The person feels an inner splintering until commitment actually occurs and the struggle to honor this commitment is undertaken. All kinds of subterfuges are used to avoid commitment: anger at the director or God, seductive behavior, procrastination, denial of the conversion experience, unconscious dishonesty about the nature and implications of the experience. Only when the directee has exhausted all avenues of escape does it become clear that the only way to resolve the inner tension is to commit wholly to the project—in other words, to surrender oneself to God.

Further, it becomes increasingly clear to the directee that a serious need for ordered religious practice is essential, that is, self-reflection, prayer, discernment, charity, virtue, personal mortification, and asceticism. These qualities are needed because they honor, revere, and support the commitment that the directee has made to live an intentional life of faith, hope, and love. The directee realizes who he or she is and who he or she wants to become. With the same clarity the directee knows that this religious practice is absolutely necessary to become a new person under the Spirit of God.

Personal Integration of God's Action

The director should be aware that the directee will hear many voices during this period: the voice of God, the voices of individual needs and fears, the voices of discouragement or encouragement, the voices from a world that resists the values and priorities of God. The director and directee both need to acquire the gift of discernment. The gifted ability to sort out such distractions and listen more attentively to the voice of God is a prime necessity for the directee. The director can help by teaching some simple techniques of discernment and collaborating with the directee.

Beginners have much to negotiate once God invites them to this higher plane—to be aware and to claim as one's own, to commit self and to integrate life around the new commitment. Each task is enormous. It is amazing and consoling to see how many people, with the aid, light, love, and presence of God and with real generosity and personal courage manage all of these tasks effectively. Their lives best support the assumption that God simply is. Without the aid and active support of a present and loving God, it would be impossible for beginning directees to accomplish so much.

Emotional Fervor,
Dry Prayer, and Spiritual Awakening

Yet, there is still much to do. Up until now God's presence has provoked significant emotional fervor that has been a deeply sustaining gift. Now the fervor will begin to diminish, even perhaps disappear altogether. This gift of devotional fervor is a kind of "bait" used by God to support the person to confront the difficult tasks and issues that need to be resolved at the beginning of the journey toward faith and commitment. The directee no longer needs the bait, and so God withdraws it. The person has been lured by God to God's self. The intense affective consolation becomes almost a distraction from further growth and development.

Once this fervor wanes or disappears, prayer, charity, and the practice of virtue take a great deal more personal effort and energy. The darker side of one's character and personality resurfaces. At times the directee feels bereft of the lived experience of God's love and presence. The directee experiences a new and deeper dryness and an almost naked fidelity to God with little emotional power to support such faithfulness. It is important for the directee to be able to share with the director the experience of repeated failure. These feelings of inadequacy also have to be accepted, appropriated, and integrated. The directee and director must work together to explore the directee's profound fear of having lost touch with God.

The directee's most important need now is to understand the meaning of what is happening, to know nothing is wrong, and to realize that this is a call to a deeper relationship with God. God has *not* abandoned the directee. On the contrary, God invites and beckons the directee to new intimacy and deeper familiarity while purifying the directee in preparation for this new familiarity and intimate presence. The directee needs to be assured that God is not being arbitrary or punitive, that the aridity or dryness is not a result of any personal fault. The directee repeatedly must hear and be convinced that God is loving, merciful, and compassionate. Often this message can be communicated by the empathic presence and understanding of the director. Reassurance occurs when the director helps the person discover the truth within—that the Spirit of God leads, that God and mysterious love abides, and that these are all wonderful gifts from God.

Since discursive and active prayer will turn painful, the directee can profit from instruction in quieter and simpler kinds of prayer that will lead to more passive, docile, and receptive responses. Often the directee will need to rely a great deal on the director. This is fine for now, but the director has to tread a very delicate balance between the director's desire to be needed and the directee's reliance on the director. Nevertheless, with the director's assistance the directee will be able to more readily accept this new path of aridity.

Over a period of time fidelity to dry prayer feeds the motivation of the person and energizes the will. Through such faithfulness the person's dependence on sensible emotion and affection in relating to God is ruptured. A deeper resting of the will in God occurs. God exposes divine mystery and goodness to the person; the person wants to rest in this goodness with a kind of gentle complacency. No longer is there an imaginative stimulation or affective activity in prayer. In large measure, the person will say, "It's awfully dry and difficult and tedious to pray, but I don't want to let go of it. I am certainly not a spiritual masochist; I want to pray, because I know in some mysterious way that my personality is being shaped by the reality of God, and my will is being bonded to the wonderful goodness of God." Such is the transformation accomplished by the Spirit of God in this time of sensory dryness.

Throughout, the directee's intense identification with emotions has been broken and/or purified. A capacity for absorption in prayer and a greater sensitivity to God's subtle action grows stronger. Now develops a far greater sensitivity to the numinous, greater and more energetic creativity, and less self-centeredness since the action of God has released some of the deeper creative energies of the personality. Ironically, the director has a strange need to remind the directee that religious sentiments will continue and that it is indeed important to experience them. The director does so not to re-create dependence, but to keep the directee acting in a conscious manner. By reminding the person of his or her affections, the director can help the person to maintain the gifts of humanity, humility, reality, and compassion to self and others. Unless the directee is rooted in reality, strange things can and often do happen. Physical and emotional problems can develop. Missing sleep or skipping meals for the sake of prayer are not uncommon. The director must be attentive to these phenomena and acknowledge them as mere temptations and aberrations.

I want to emphasize that this pattern of growth and development happens to people in all walks of life, especially to people who take their lives and their God seriously. It is not restricted to contemplative religious or clerics. This is the ordinary stuff of life and commitment, the stuff of faith development and ordinary spiritual direction.

What does a director do with the directee during this time of intense spiritual awakening? What does the director do for the directee? It is important to create an accepting and trusting environment in which the directee can share a wealth of experience. Both the director and the directee should consistently center their conversation on the simple awareness of the presence and love of God and the manifold ways in which these qualities are demonstrated experientially. Together they must avoid analysis of the experience. Analysis is discursive and centers on oneself, not on the presence and love of God. Many of the aids of earlier development, such as journal keeping, are not advisable at this time, because they move the focus away from God. The entire focus of prayer and experience is on the simple realization that God is lovingly with the person.

The person can rely on more intuitive ways to cooperate as fully as possible with the Spirit of God, rather than developing rational alternatives. One does not abandon rationality, but one can trust instinct and intuition more readily. The inner action of the Spirit eliminates even the minimalist obstacles to interior and spirited decision making. The purpose of the director is to affirm these intuitive and noncognitive ways of knowing, reacting, and deciding. Such affirmation by the director assures the directee that this new mode of spiritual discretion or discernment is accurate and trustworthy.

Where does this activity of God leave the person? In a sort of limbo of activity! The person is indeed adrift. There will be renewed anxiety because the memory, intellect, imagination, and sense perceptions are not functioning as they had before. The person seems caught in darkness, emptiness, an interior vacuum or void. These phenomena, in part, mark the beginning of a final and very difficult period of purification undertaken by God.

Final Period of Purification

New temptations of excessive pleasure, lust, religious scruples, and neurotic guilt come into consciousness. In a sense, God is ordering the unconscious of the directee. As clinicians and therapists attest, a great deal of life is lived from unconscious motivations, drives, and desires. We make or avoid many important tasks and decisions based on motives, fears, anxieties, and taboos that are not conscious or immediately available to us. Now God gently begins to expose these unconscious movements—our deepest desires—and arrange them in a new way for our well-being.

In prayer and during the preceding processes of growth and development, the person has learned that God will not satisfy these self-centered needs and desires. In earlier stages of faith growth the person moved to the limits of his or her personal strength and capacity for believing, hoping, and loving. Now the light of the Spirit of God illuminates the directee's unconscious. The light of God alternates with periods of intense darkness. The contrast and alternation is a painful but transforming reality.

This is an extraordinarily graced time for both the director and the directee, but it is also a difficult and painful time. A great deal of negative unconscious feelings in the directee emerge, a dark void colored by crazy desires and deep fears. The director should encourage the person to speak about these anxieties, agitations, obsessions, and fantasies. If they are left unexpressed, they will become overwhelming and frightening to the directee. When these emotions are expressed by the directee, they lose their negative quality; they begin to appear more manageable.

It can be very difficult and, at times, painful for the directee to acknowledge these feelings. They can be embarrassing and humiliating, such as when the directee realizes the existence of incestuous desires or fantasizes about a parent or sibling. The director has to be compassionately present to help bring this material to consciousness and encourage expression, no matter what its content. The cathartic effect of verbal expression is often quite incredible.

The directee must utilize the psychic strength of the director during this painful time of personal and passive purification. Personal anxiety must be alleviated by the dialogue in the direction session. It is important for rationality to win over the wild assaults of the unconscious. Thus the director may make strength and rationality available to the directee. Even here, though, the same kind of discretion must be exercised, lest the director try to serve his or her own needs.

If the experience is difficult for the directee, it also taxes the resources of the director. Since the directee may lean on the director, the director may well feel drained, used, and debilitated. The director will need more rest, more time for prayer, more personal preparation for direction meetings, and more patience. The director will have to work hard to maintain compassion and presence in these meetings because the directee will likely languish in self-pity, self-hate, or deep fear and anxiety. Both parties must work together to develop specific plans and directions to control the seemingly uncontrollable sensations, fears, and desires of the directee. The important thing to remember is to persevere and constantly make an effort to understand the unconscious. Any actual success or failure is immaterial.

The danger here is that the directee will begin to think that his or her personhood is falling apart, that he or she is losing control of life or work, prayer or relationships. The directee needs immediate assurance that such is not the case. To alleviate this feeling of despair, the director must continue to be supportive, present, understanding, and affirming. The director also must be knowledgeable about the particular dynamics of the experience in order to provide an authentic ring of confidence.

The director must not be afraid to suggest using distractions and diversions. Contrary to perception, these activities do not support or encourage escapist behavior. In fact, the more the person tries to escape from an experiential situation, the more intense the experience actually becomes. The director encourages recreative behavior specifically so that the person can be rested and able to face the negative forces of the unconscious. Therefore, any physical or psychological help that will alleviate the negative force emanating from the unconscious is to be recommended by the director. Often such help proves to be beneficial for the directee.

It is important to remember that the sense of darkness or emptiness that inevitably develops is a form of profound interior transformation or restructuring. It often takes the shape or form of an unspecified distress. It may be partly physical, partly emotional, partly psychological, or partly spiritual. Usually the directee does not understand what is happening. Attempts at analysis generally cause further turmoil and anxiety. Rather than wrestling cognitively with the experience, it is better for the director to merely appropriate the event and be present, being alert for the subtle presence of God.

In this setting God simply requires faith from the person— a quality of faith that exists, grows, and intensifies without any significant experiential data or any signs of the existence or presence of the living and loving God. God provides for the person the arena or forum, the holy place, in which faith can grow intensely. Because God provokes it and is deeply present, it is important for the director to encourage the directee to enter into and be present to the experience.

The directee experiences a time of immense crisis, turmoil, and personal conflict. The crisis is actually precipitated by the brightness of contemplative light that the directee is receiving from the Spirit of God. This light is *too* bright; it is very much like the brightness of the sun, at once both alluring and attractive, but so intense it causes temporary or even permanent blindness. To the directee the proximity of the light and wisdom of God actually seems like darkness because of its overwhelming intensity. It is the kind of divine light that purges and purifies even as it illuminates.

Only God knows what lies buried in the unconscious or what needs to be ordered and illuminated in the character, temperament, or personality of the directee. The duration of this purifying experience is solely at God's discretion and under the guidance of God's Spirit. Radical transformation of the personality is affected by the Spirit; it can only occur in real time and history. The effects of the transformation need ample opportunity in order to be rooted deeply in the personality. The entire process may endure for a great length of time. In fact, the experience is often so painful that even a brief duration seems interminably long. By this time, it should be clear that God does not invite a person to such an experience without a divine promise that it will lead to a deeper union with God. Seldom does a person come to this kind of purification without being called to it by the Spirit of God. The invitation is tantamount to a guarantee that the process will be completed by God and that a new order of intimacy in the relationship with God will be established.

The directee who is loved by God into this experience is a rare breed indeed. The person is aware of individual beliefs, hopes, and loves through the deeper power and love of the Spirit of God within. There is a continual experiential realization of the presence and activity of God. The person has discovered in his or her own spirit the deepest mysteries of personhood, spiritual integration, and soul. The person grows in the awareness of profound contemplative activity within—a quality of presence of God that was previously obscured in the empty darkness of the unconscious. Inner and wordless prayer can now coexist on peaceful terms without disturbing the personality by either producing ecstasy or darkness. God has claimed the entirety of the person, even as the person has appropriated the deepest facets of his or her personality.

These various processes of purification and integration have transformed and ordered the personality at the most profound level possible. The person is now complete and can be wholly present to God. The only missing element is a lived assurance, tested over a period of time that the use of personal abilities—memory, intellect, imagination, will—is now purified. The person needs to know that such activities are no longer an obstacle in seeking God, but rather a gift that can be used in the purest pursuit of the love, presence, and service of the living God.

This graced and gifted person needs the time and leisure to grow in the assurance and confirmation of what God has accomplished. Time is also needed to become accustomed to the situation. Moreover, the person will need to seek creative outlets for the new and renewed energies. Finally, time will be needed to explore the new dimension of interpersonal relationships that have been opened by the transforming action of the Spirit of God.

The director must realize that he or she is dispensable. The director must assure the directee that the living God within is sufficient and that spiritual direction in its former sense is no longer necessary. This realization can be difficult for some directors who want or need to cling to their directees. Because the directee is alert to the activity of God, even when it is subtle or sophisticated, the directee's sense of inner direction is almost flawless. Consequently, there is no need for a spiritual director. All that a director can do for the directee is confirm the decisions that the directee has made and allow a forum for the directee's experiences.

The director can help the person to avoid spiritual pride. Spiritual pride, you may recall, occurs when the person begins to think, feel, and act as if the extraordinary gift of God was somehow owed. Much subtlety is involved here; the director should learn to be alert to the various forms that this "sin" can assume and point it out clearly and immediately to the directee if it ever surfaces. If this be the extent of the director's service to the directee, it would still be a great gift.

Most people whom God has invited to enter this marvelous kind of intimacy will still want, though they will not need, a spiritual friend, a director, or a companion who, with them, will recognize the great work that God has done, will praise God for it, and celebrate regularly with acts of thanksgiving. In other words, the relationship between the director and the directee can still continue, but its quality and function will change significantly.

Conclusion

In these reflections I have tried to create a portrait of the inner processes of growth in awareness of and development of one's relationship with God. My initial intention was to describe a variety of categories or types of directees and a process of development from one stage of life in the Spirit to another. I have, I believe, accomplished this task, but I have also found it necessary to include reflections on the spiritual director—things to do or avoid, signs to watch for, various levels of experience of the directee. After all, spiritual direction is a relationship. It is impossible to discuss and reflect on one partner in the relationship without offering some parallel reflections on the other. I have also struggled to avoid the theoretical in favor of practical suggestions for both the director and the directee. My deepest hope is, of course, that these reflections will be helpful for anyone involved in spiritual direction, either as director or directee. With this in mind, I now turn to particular types of directees, their more particularized needs, and what specifically a director can do with and for these people as they continue on their path and journey to God.

Further Reading

Katherine Marie Dyckman, S.N.J.M., and L. Patrick Carroll, S.J., *Inviting the Mystic, Supporting the Prophet* (Mahwah, N.J.: Paulist Press, 1981).

Rose Page, O.C.D., "Direction in the Various Stages of Spiritual Development," *Contemplative Review* 12 (fall 1979): 11–18.

2

Some Particular Types of Directees and Their Needs

Not many directors will have the privilege or gift to direct people in the latter stages of faith, growth, and development. In well over twenty-five years of spiritual direction, I have known and directed only four people who have entered the dark night of the spirit and emerged as authentic contemplatives. Perhaps it is my own limitations as a spiritual director that help explain this situation. Or perhaps the Spirit of God leads people to spiritual directors who can experientially and accurately guide and direct them out of their own gifted development. Therefore, since I am not (yet) such a contemplative, the Spirit has not brought these people to me for spiritual direction. Further, I know from discussion and conversation with countless other directors that few of them have had the honor either. Thus, I can only conclude that it will be the rare director who has had the great gift to direct such people.

Even so, this conclusion does not excuse any director from continuing to pursue and explore the gifts of prayer and spiritual growth that God has given him or her and from collaborating with and responding generously to those gifts, whatever they may be. Nor does it excuse a director from determining the best way to deal with a person called by God, even though the director may not be touched by the Spirit of God. It may well be that there would be many more such gifted people if spiritual directors were more knowledgeable and competent in their ministry! The vast majority of the directees with whom most directors will journey will be people of fidelity, whose life and prayer is indeed graced and gifted, but still growing and toward a much deeper union and familiarity with God. It is such people and their particular needs that I now want to consider.

Five Types of Directees

There are five types of directees: (1) people who are entering spiritual direction for the first time; (2) people who have experienced a religious conversion; (3) people who are experiencing the dryness and aridity of fidelity over a long period of time; (4) people who are living a contemplative lifestyle, whatever their growth in prayer and faith may be; and (5) people who live a kind of roller-coaster faith life with periods of intense prayer followed by equally long periods of no prayer at all. Each of these groups has their own specific needs in spiritual direction. As I did in the previous chapter, I will meld my reflections about director and directee together. Rather than enter into any extended conversation about the theory of direction, I will describe the type of person based on personal experience, and then I will note what role the director can play in each situation to meet the very specific needs of the directees. My intention is to be as practical and experiential as possible.

Directees Beginning
Spiritual Direction for the First Time

People starting spiritual direction for the first time fall into a very special class of directees. For the director they represent that new and mysterious other who can bring either good news or bad news. This type of directee is a wholly unknown entity: the director cannot even make an educated guess about the meaning of the relationship or about the directee's growth and development. There is indeed something awesome here—a mixture of fascination and fear—for both director and directee when a new relationship of direction begins.

Even the most competent, experienced, and qualified directors feel some anxiety when beginning a new spiritual direction relationship, especially when the new directee is entering spiritual direction for the first time. A new directee's emotions can vary from immaturity and lack of sophistication in spiritual growth and development to the most advanced stages of prayer and intimacy with God. All that both the director and directee know is that they are beginning a new, mysterious, challenging, and holy relationship and that the Spirit of God will use the director as a guide, companion, and fellow sojourner with this person.

It is of paramount importance that the director be prepared to begin this new and intriguing relationship. First, there must be intense prayer for oneself and the directee prior to beginning the relationship and immediately before the initial interview. The director prays for alertness, openness, illumination, trust, patience, the capacity to listen, tempering of personal fear and anxiety, and a welcoming and hospitable reaction to the new directee. The director also prays for the well-being of the directee. This prayer should be in the form of a general prayer of petition, that is, that the loving God will give the person any and every gift that will enable him or her to find God in peace and in truth. The director does not yet know the directee's needs and so can only pray in a very general way. Thus, the director prays intently for the quality of this new relationship to be under the guidance, gift, and inspiration of the Holy Spirit.

Second, the director must also resort to a process of self-reflection and self-examination. The director must bring to consciousness the darker side of his or her personality and temperament, as well as the particular gifts that will be put at the service of the new relationship. New relationships of spiritual direction are always moments of new truth and new personal honesty for the director.

Many personal idiosyncrasies of the director can impede the process of spiritual direction. These can be especially detrimental with someone who has not had spiritual direction before. The director should, therefore, call to awareness any personal sinfulness and discuss how this sinfulness has been healed by the saving love and mercy of God. Behavior such as personal blindness, prejudice, or personal hang-ups must also be acknowledged by the director and brought to consciousness but in such a way that will not be destructive to the directee.

Finally, the director must be very careful to nurture the appropriate atmosphere for a first-time directee. The director must strive for an atmosphere of hospitality. More and more, people are looking for a safe place where they can feel comfortable and unafraid. So much of modern life communicates that the world and other human beings are essentially hostile. Early in life most of us learn to be suspicious and distrustful, to expect as normal the difficult, the devious, and the distasteful. Social and professional competition are the order of the day. People have been used, abused, manipulated, and oppressed in various relationships from the familial to the ecclesial, the professional to the personal. Many people emerge from this kind of life-context as they begin the new relationship of spiritual direction. Their first impressions often determine how the relationship will develop and prosper. Therefore, the atmosphere that is created by the director at the very beginning of the relationship is of utmost importance.

In the course of this new relationship, the directee will be invited to share with the director personal insights no one else knows. Such an exchange can only occur in an atmosphere of safety, trust, and mutual personal care—in short, in an atmosphere of hospitality where the person is secure enough to share precious secrets.

Let us presume that the director has prepared for meeting someone who is beginning spiritual direction for the first time and that this same director has engaged in prayer for the directee and in serious self-reflection and self-examination. We can also hope that the director has created an atmosphere of Christian hospitality in which the directee can be assured of safety and security that will facilitate conversation and significant self-revelation. What else is needed? What must the director attend to in such a person? What are some of the tasks and issues that must be addressed at the beginning of this relationship? What help can and should the director offer at this time?

Probably the most important task is that of personal awareness. People begin spiritual direction for a great many reasons. Perhaps the most overriding reason is because they have become aware of something new and mysterious in their life. Something is happening to them that causes confusion, anxiety, fear, and anger or, paradoxically, evokes joy or pleasure. They cannot understand, manage, or control something in their consciousness. What is important is that they have become *aware* of their new reality. They are seeking help in appropriating and integrating this awareness into their lived experience. Ultimately, it is such awareness that most often leads one to seek spiritual direction. Thus, the director must point the directee in the appropriate direction.

Direction, then, invariably begins by helping the person be aware of whatever experience(s) has led him or her to the director. It is very important that the director receive this self-revelation with care, reverence, and utmost seriousness no matter how strange, trivial, or unreal it may seem. The reverence of the director allows and encourages the beginning directee to become more aware and more alert to this experience and to determine its value, meaning, and purpose in living a fuller life in God. Without such awareness, everything else in direction will remain pure notion, a kind of "head-trip," or a fantasy that has little or no grounding in reality.

Although it may appear simple and clear, so easy to accomplish and achieve, this awareness eludes many people. Many individuals live on the surface of their deepest experience; their lives are truly and tragically superficial. They have little or no access to the precious and profound dimensions of their life. They are simply unaware: they do not understand what is happening to them and how it is affecting them. For this reason, I maintain that coming to rudimentary awareness of personal experience is a great gift and one of the first and most important signs that the Spirit of God is working in one's life. It is also the fundamental task of the director to acknowledge this sign when working with someone in direction for the first time.

Attention and awareness are the very stuff of early spiritual direction. Until one begins to attend to and become aware of what is actually happening, especially within, no real growth in faith is possible. When awareness is low, the directee's personal progress is minimal, because growth depends on the level of awareness of God's action and the choice of responses that are appropriate to that action. The importance that the person eventually puts on such awareness will almost certainly determine the value put on spiritual direction. If there is a lack of awareness, if the person is uninterested in cultivating a habit of personal sensitivity, then spiritual direction is likely to degenerate into giving advice, problem solving, or answering theoretical questions that have little, if anything, to do with the deepest realities of the directee's life.

At this early stage of the relationship, the director must also be careful not to trivialize the experience of the directee. It may take a great deal of patience, presence, and compassion to share with a beginning directee biographical details and explore the reasons and lived experiences that led to spiritual direction. This kind of presence persuades the directee that the "catalyst" experience is indeed worth relating and that it is very much the pearl of great price. Slowly, the directee begins to realize that life and experience are the arena in which the Spirit of God works.

In addition to helping the beginner to become alert to foundational religious experiences, the director should also clarify the limits of the relationship. Obviously, both director and directee have real expectations. It is far better to discuss these expectations with one another at the beginning and thus avoid any frustration as the relationship progresses. Clarification has the further advantage in that it helps the directee to become more aware of personal motives for starting direction. It thus becomes another way for the director to promote the kind of awareness and attention that are necessary. It can also provide the director with the opportunity to share with the person his or her conception of direction and the implications of the spiritual direction process. It allows the director to examine at length the role he or she plays or the kind of demands the director feels can be made on the directee if the relationship is to flourish and be productive.

In these ways, the director can actually direct the person, that is, point to methods of praying and reflecting while noting experiences that will be helpful. As a director I find it very important to know how the person prays early on in the relationship. Consequently, I ask the directee to pray with specific ideas that have come up in our initial conversation. For example, I might point to some scriptural material that seems relevant or encourage the directee to pray about some of the things we have discussed. In a subsequent meeting, then, I would explore with the directee both the fruit of the prayer and the mode, manner, or style of prayer. It is far more important for the director to come to understand the person's gift of prayer than to hear about the insights, ideas, or illuminations that the person might have experienced in prayer. In fact, it is the personal gift of prayer that is usually most indicative of the actual workings of the Spirit of God within the person.

It is also of utmost importance to reassure the directee, particularly one who has never had direction before, that there is no sacrosanct or canonized way of praying that must be followed. Though the person might indeed have a notable history of personal prayer prior to beginning direction, the directee generally worries about the "rightness" or appropriateness of his or her current style or gift of prayer. The directee needs to know that every prayer is unique and valuable. The director's reassurance gives the person "permission" to follow the urgings, promptings, and movements of the Spirit of God in prayer.

Early on, it is valuable to plan on some ongoing evaluation of the relationship. Once expectations have been clarified and there is ample time to see if they are actually being met, then the directee should have the opportunity to evaluate what has happened and what might continue to happen. Together the director and directee should plan a time for evaluation—perhaps after seven or eight conversations, for example. Clearly the directee should be given the freedom to withdraw from the relationship if it has not proved to be helpful for spiritual development and growth. In addition, new expectations can be clarified as they continue to emerge in the relationship.

After a period of seven or eight meetings the director should be able to make some tentative evaluation about the religious and spiritual identity of the directee. It will now be easier for the director to understand the psychoreligious state of the person. The real issues of the directee now become more clear to the director in a way, perhaps, that are not yet apparent to the directee. During the evaluation period, the director should be able to elaborate some of these insights for the directee in a helpful and illuminating way. Quite often, such feedback proves to be one of the major advantages of the entire evaluative procedure.

Typical Issues of Directees
Beginning Direction for the First Time

God is a God of freedom who collaborates with the person to optimize or maximize personal freedom. This means that the Spirit of God labors with the person in a process of personal liberation, so that the person can love more freely and return the gift of freedom, caring, and service to God and one's neighbor. What's more, people are generally unfree in four or five areas of life. Fear, anger, depression, sexuality, and authority are, I believe, the areas or issues of life that most inhibit people; they are extremely problematic and difficult for people to handle. Depending on the quality of the relationship and the trust that actually develops between the director and a new directee, these areas may enter the conversation of spiritual direction. Even if they do not, the director can learn a great deal about the directee by confronting them. As a part of ordinary, everyday human experience, one expects these areas of life to be revealed and discussed by anyone seeking direction or trying to determine the meaning, purpose, pattern, and value of life. If they are consistently overlooked by a directee, the director should keep a mental note for future reference. Such omissions could well indicate areas of resistance or blindness.

Where do these unfreedoms lie? How can a director approach them with someone who is just beginning spiritual direction? The Spirit of God is working with the person to deepen personal freedom in these important areas of life and relationships. Let us look briefly, then, at each, particularly as they surface in the directee who is just beginning spiritual direction.

FEAR. The greatest obstacle to personal freedom is fear. Fear makes us do what we do not want to do and often inhibits us from doing what is in our best interest. Fear wears many masks and takes a great variety of shapes and forms—fear of failure, fear of personal rejection, fear of increased responsibility for one's life, fear of others' expectations. Some of us fear success, intimacy, even God. Others fear competition, sibling rivalry, parental pressures. Fear can be very strong, as in a kind of terror, or very subtle, as in a low-grade anxiety. It is intrusive and pervasive; it controls both personal behavior and communal activity.

Most people do not speak readily or easily of their fears. It is humiliating and embarrassing to do so. Some people find it difficult either because they are unaware of or out of touch with their fears, even the great, debilitating, and oppressive ones. Others have denied or suppressed their fears. It takes much effort and gentle probing on the part of the director to bring these deep-seated fears to the surface. Denial and suppression especially affects men who are just beginning spiritual direction. Contemporary American society conditions men either to intellectualize their fears or to deny them completely. It is therefore exceedingly difficult to evoke from men an honest awareness of their personal fears. Whatever the reason, the issue of fear must be addressed at some point with a person beginning spiritual direction. To not do so would be a major impediment to personal freedom.

What can a director do when confronting such a situation? What aid can a director offer as a directee begins to discuss the fears that control and inhibit his or her freedom? The director must make available the gifts of empathetic understanding and presence. This form of compassion allows the director to be present to the directee without any threat of negative judgment frightening the directee. A positive regard for the directee that is actually felt by the director and directly communicated to the person is absolutely crucial. Furthermore, the director must let the directee feel accepted and revered, not in spite of the fears but because of them! It is often very helpful—even salutary, healing, and redemptive— for the director to share honestly his or her own fears as well as coping mechanisms, so that they no longer control life and behavior. Also, prayer for light and deliverance from fear can be encouraged. A directee can find hope and courage in the Word of God, by realizing how often God raises people out of their fear and delivers them from the most frightening realities of life. This kind of prayer, along with the empathy and encouragement of the director, can do a great deal to help the person handle the dark mystery of fear.

Freedom begins with naming one's fears. The directee must identify the fears, own them, and react to them in new and creative ways. Often a person struggles with the unnamed and the mysterious; the fears seem enormous and completely unmanageable. Naming the fears brings them into the realm of the intelligible. Owning the fears involves the rational and emotional acceptance of realities as fears. They belong to the individual. By owning the fears the directee allows the fears into awareness and consciousness. The full impact of the fear is now realized and felt. This response is the most difficult part of the process, but it is the only sure way to achieve deeper personal freedom. Finally, the person must creatively choose strategies to cope with and alleviate the fears through new ways of acting, withdrawing, relating, avoiding, and praying.

ANGER. Anger is another reality that significantly inhibits personal freedom. It too deserves serious consideration during the early stages of spiritual direction; it can also be an important factor with people who have had a a variety of experiences of direction. We live in a socioreligious culture in which anger has been severely criticized and tabooed. We are faced with a strong, learned moral bias or prejudice that presumes that anger is morally reprehensible. For the most part anger is socially unacceptable. Most of us avoid people who display anger publicly or who are temperamentally inclined to violent expressions of anger. Such people make us anxious and uneasy, even when their anger is mature and righteous. The honest expression of anger becomes almost impossible because of the social, religious, and moral strictures we have implicitly or explicitly placed on it. The situation has become so bad that unexpressed anger is probably the most significant and problematic reality in contemporary American religious community life.

A number of important things should be noted about anger that can be especially useful for someone beginning spiritual direction. The director should gently communicate various insights to the directee to help diffuse the painful anger that can block expressions of affectivity and emotion. First, the director must help the directee to recognize and understand that anger is amoral, neither right nor wrong, good nor bad. It is a body/spirit reaction—a felt reaction—to a variety of stimuli. It only becomes moral when the person decides how to deal with it, how to express it, and what to do about it. How can the director communicate this most effectively to the directee, particularly one who appears deeply embarrassed when expressing anger? Probably the most effective way is to encourage the person to contemplate the Gospels, particularly those episodes in which Jesus himself displays significant anger, such as the cleansing of the temple, where the anger of Jesus is so intense that it involves physical violence, or the encounter at Caesarea Philippi where Jesus becomes visibly and publicly angry with Peter, his very close and dear personal friend. Gradually, the power of the Word of God opens the directee to the truth and reality that anger is not intrinsically wrong, that there are times when it is the most human and appropriate reaction to a given situation.

Second, a director can explore the meaning of personal anger with the directee and help the person to understand what happens in any experience of anger, however intense it may be. It is somewhat of an oversimplification, but true nonetheless, that anger is the felt experience of frustration. Basically, the person experiences and feels the frustration of some need or personal expectation. When need-satisfaction is blocked or expectations of self or others are frustrated or violated, the felt frustration is one of anger. The best example is the enraged infant lying in a crib and crying out of deep frustration: generally the child either needs to be fed or expects to be changed. The frustration of this need or expectation is displayed as infantile rage.

Again, how can a director help a directee to handle and resolve frustration? Since we live in a culture and society that equates reduction or denial of needs with personal human maturation, people who know and feel their needs often seem immature. This can be embarrassing for some people; they realize that they have personal needs, yet they have been taught to believe that they should *not* have such needs. They can either deny their needs or leave them largely unmet and unsatisfied. The situation can lead to a low-grade anger that is often very debilitating. It is important for the director to help the directee recognize, accept, and satisfy creatively the real needs that are felt and experienced by the directee. Otherwise the needs will persist and continue to fester, demanding immediate action. The person then often seeks devious and unhealthy ways to satisfy such needs and feels great guilt and discomfort. Only when the needs are named and recognized, owned and accepted can they be seen as a gift, and only then can the person engage in life-giving and creative ways of satisfying them. The director can help the directee to face his or her needs and thus reduce the felt frustration that is personal anger.

In addition, the director may have to help the directee address thwarted personal expectations as well as frustrated expectations of oneself and others. Usually the expectations are overblown, often considerably beyond any reasonable possibility or hope of fulfillment. Doomed to failure and frustration, these expectations predictably stimulate anger and resentment. Here the director can help the directee gain a sense of reality—a set of expectations that are more limited, more real, and more readily satisfied. Facing reality is a difficult task, because people cling to the myths and misguided perceptions of themselves. They hesitate to surrender familiar expectations—no matter how far-fetched—and replace them with a more realistic and healthier set. They easily defend expectations that are often very attractive, commendable, and even quite noble. People internalize the myth that it takes only a little more courage, a little more generosity, or a little more support from others for them to live up to their expectations. It takes patience, presence, some wisdom, and much perseverance for a director to make a directee realize how destructive such exaggerated expectations can be, but it is well worth the effort because it can lead to a much deeper sense of personal peace and significantly alleviate long-term and destructive anger.

More often than not people will expect from others what they really expect from themselves. Much anger is involved here, because so few people can meet the unstated and exaggerated expectations that are placed on them. This kind of frustration, when others cannot or do not meet what one thinks are realistic and legitimate expectations of them, is the source of much pain, hurt, frustration, and long-term unexpressed anger. These violated expectations often have a long history, a festering ugly quality that distresses and confuses the person. It is too facile a solution merely to suggest that the person learn to lessen such expectations, especially after they have caused deep pain in the past. From personal experience I have found the healing of memories, in which the person is led by the Spirit of God to share violated expectations with the director in the healing presence of the loving God, to be the most effective response. This prayerful exercise often defuses the anger that can result from painfully frustrated expectations. Having said this, however, I must add one important warning: a director should not begin the healing of memories process unless he or she possesses the skills to understand and handle their implications. This kind of emotional healing involves many subtle psychological dynamics. To begin the process with a directee when one is ignorant of these dynamics is both irresponsible and dangerous.

DEPRESSION. Depression is a third important area of unfreedom. It may sound strange to address depression in a set of reflections about spiritual direction. But I think it is almost unavoidable to do so, because in contemporary American society depression has been called the common cold of the clinical professions. Depression has reached almost epidemic proportions in all sectors of American society—young and old, rich and poor, male and female, religious and lay. At some point the majority of people who begin spiritual direction will be afflicted by at least a mild form of psychological depression. This may mean that they will be unable to think or talk about anything other than how bad they feel. A dark pall covers every dimension of life. It infects work, leisure, relationships, and prayer. It erodes and contaminates everything it touches. In its clinical forms it can be so painful that it leads some people to self-destructive or even suicidal behavior. In its more mild manifestations it can induce paralysis since it is so often characterized by chronic and painful feelings of utter helplessness and hopelessness.

Depression, more than any other obstacle to human freedom, demands a competent and experienced director. The director must be able to recognize the signs and symptoms of depression and know his or her own limitations. Often all a director can do is urge the directee to begin psychological counseling or therapy. The director must be able to recognize the difference between severe depression and its milder manifestations. The differences are often quite subtle. Thus the director needs considerable expertise if called upon to guide someone suffering from a major depression.

What should a director look for in someone suspected of suffering from chronic or acute depression? What are the danger signs of depression? The physical symptoms usually connected with acute depression include insomnia, irregularity, dietary disorders, and inexplicable fatigue. Feelings of helplessness and hopelessness about one or more aspects or dimensions of life are also quite common as well as a general lack of interest in anything (nothing sparks enthusiasm or excitement); an increasing disregard for personal appearance; a form of substance abuse or addictive behavior, particularly food or alcohol abuse; and some spiritual "disabilities" that are largely perceptual (God is harsh, judgmental, or punitive). Certainly, prayer will not be an adequate remedy, because it already is colored by personal distaste and notable dryness.

Some or all of these symptoms can indicate to the director the presence of depression. The director will have to weigh carefully the intensity of the symptoms. Only by thoroughly exploring the signs will the director be able to help the person and know when it is appropriate to suggest seeking professional psychological or psychiatric intervention. A major indicator of long-term and low-grade depression is the verbal self-presentation of the person. The person who chronically criticizes him- or herself, who seldom has anything good to say about the self, who caricatures or downgrades the self as inept or without value—such a person is almost certainly dealing with a long-standing history of personal depression. It helps if the director gently brings this verbal pattern of self-depreciation to the person's attention and insists that the person not engage in verbal self-abuse while in session. If the director allows the directee to continue self-erosive and self-abusive language, then the director is actually collaborating with the very dynamics that support depression. Simply being made aware of a verbal pattern of self-abuse goes a long way toward alleviating low-grade depression.

Presuming that the director is alert to the reality of depression and knows the differences between the mild and more severe forms, what can the director do when the situation is one that falls within his or her personal competence? Can the director do anything to aid the person who is debilitated by low-grade, chronic feelings of incompetence or ineptitude? More often than not the reason for affective depression is diminished or eroded self-esteem. The person has either not enjoyed the experience of an adequate sense of personal identity or self-esteem has been battered by the shocks and difficulties of life. This situation really involves introjected anger, that is, personal frustration in which the directee is both the subject and object of his or her anger. Much affective and emotional energy is employed, but it is used by the person in a self-destructive way. The perceptions of the individual are askew, since all personal feelings are negative, critical, and threatening. Tunnel vision results.

The person can only note and react to what is wrong with him- or herself. Any positive data gets filtered out, because it does not fit the person's negative self-concept.

Often this common type of depression has a long history that reaches back into adolescence and family life to a time when personal identity and self-esteem were forged. Frequently, the "performance principle" in American life is the chief reason for this phenomenon. In many American families affirmation, acceptance, and affection are measured out to children in proportion to their social, academic, or athletic accomplishments. It may not always be a conscious act, but it is pervasive. Children are stretched to maximal performance, while parents often achieve their own emotional security and self-esteem from the good behavior and performance of their offspring. In most cases the children exhaust the limits of personal ability. They do not or cannot meet the exaggerated performance expectations of their parents nor can they compete with their siblings. Within the family, emotional affirmation is diminished or withheld. The child, especially in adolescence, interprets this lack of affection and absence of affirmation as a slap in the face. After all, affection and affirmation are the basic ingredients in building an adequate sense of identity and self-esteem during this crucial period of personal psychological development. The depressed feelings continue into adulthood, with such individuals leading a diminished and truncated life.

Chronically depressed persons do need, and some actually seek, spiritual direction. They are often beginners who have experienced dealing with the personal and painful problems of depression. How can a director help such a person? The task of the director is affirmation, positive-enforcement, acceptance, perceptual change, and assistance in building a sense of self-esteem within the individual that is true to the reality of one's personhood, not based on mere performance or accomplishment. The work to be done is delicate and subtle because it can readily be infected by dishonesty or hyperbole by the director or dependence and attachment by the directee. The director must consistently, patiently, and constantly remember that he or she is God's instrument in affirming and accepting the person. In no way can the director allow affirmation or human acceptance to replace the affirming and mysterious presence that brought the person to begin spiritual direction. This realization insures that the director will stay honest in the affirmation and positive acceptance of the directee.

The director must also be aware of exaggerated attachments by the directee. Certainly if the director is affirming and accepting of a person who is mildly and chronically depressed, some dependence is inevitable and therefore acceptable—at least for a brief time. The director must delicately weigh and judge how much dependence to allow and how much to encourage. The director's judgment must always be made on the basis of what is good, beneficial, and liberating for the directee, not to flatter the ego of the director. Because of the situation's sensitive nature and the potentially harmful effect that a mistake in judgment can have on the directee, it is advisable for the director to seek counsel from another qualified director or from a professional counselor or therapist.

Further, the director can assist directees by helping them to understand and modify their image of God. Where there is a situation of long-term depression, God is often perceived as very threatening—the extension or projection of the non-affirming, judgmental, and punitive parent. Generally, the only way that this situation can be remedied is through quiet prayer that allows the person to explore the experience that led to spiritual direction. Only the experience of the God who loves, affirms, and accepts unconditionally can confirm one's sense of personal identity and self-esteem. Oftentimes the way to aid a person to this new sense of self is by experiencing beauty, particularly in nature, music, or self-sacrifice.

Finally, as a matter of professional integrity, every director should become knowledgeable about the dynamics and symptoms of depression and, especially, the forms of depression that can be treated by an "amateur," for when it comes to treating severe depression most spiritual directors are indeed amateurs. They can, therefore, do great damage to a seriously depressed directee if they are not mindful of their own limitations. I cannot emphasize this strongly enough.

SEXUALITY. Another cause of unfreedom for people beginning spiritual direction is the matter of sexuality. Of all the issues I have discussed, this one deserves the most careful and reverent consideration. Nothing creates so much turmoil, ambiguity, confusion, and anxiety for most people—adolescents and adults alike—as does one's sexuality. It is an area of life ordinarily surrounded by social, religious, moral, and general human concern since so many social fears and taboos, moral strictures and admonitions, religious insights and prohibitions, political challenges and difficulties cluster around human sexuality. At the same time, it is the most normal and most mysterious of realities. It provokes fear and fascination, curiosity and exploration, personal growth and regression. It determines the quality of all our interpersonal relationships, characterizing them as either faithful or promiscuous, committed or seductive, liberating or manipulative, affirming or abusive. It marks every cell of our bodies and is largely determinative of who we are before God and other human beings.

For a person beginning spiritual direction, issues of sexuality may be among the more problematic areas of life, and yet it is an issue that usually enters the spiritual direction dialogue only after a long period of time. It takes much trust and confidence in another person to be able to discuss something as personal, delicate, and intimate as one's sexual development and growth. A director can handle the situation in a number of ways. First, I urge discretion and patience. Any effort to intrude will almost certainly be met with strong resistance and defensiveness by the directee. If the directee is struggling with sexual issues, sexual identity, or the quality of personal relationships, and, if the director proves him- or herself to be trustworthy, personally integrated, and affirming, then the topic of sexuality will eventually enter the spiritual direction conversation. There really is no way to force the issue, even when the director is certain that it is causing major unfreedom in the directee.

Second, the director must guard against any hint of sexual voyeurism during the spiritual direction process. People become notably vulnerable in spiritual direction. They are candid and forthcoming about themselves. Unfortunately, an unscrupulous spiritual director can take advantage of the directee's vulnerability and use the self-revelation as a way to control or manipulate. People, including spiritual directors, generally have a high degree of sexual curiosity. Thus, spiritual directors can use the direction relationship to satisfy their curiosity in a voyeuristic fashion. To reiterate, any allusion to such matters must be avoided at all costs, because it threatens the holistic well-being of the directee— the well-being to which both the director and directee are dedicated and committed.

Third, the director must personally have achieved a fair degree of personal maturation and sexual integration. If the director is uncomfortable discussing sexual issues with the directee—that is, if sexuality produces feelings of fear, personal turmoil, and anxiety within the director—then honest and open communication between the two parties becomes impossible. Even if these emotions are purely subliminal, they may lead the directee to believe that something is deeply wrong with him- or herself rather than that it being a personal issue for the director to resolve.

Finally, a brief word must be said concerning the sexual dynamics of the relationship between director and directee. It is a deeply human relationship and, as such, it will be marked by the realities of human sexuality. Furthermore, it is a relationship of increasing trust, self-revelation, self-exposure, and profound vulnerability. A growing sexual attraction between director and directee may also occur, although usually either party is only marginally conscious of it. Directees may engage in some form of seductive behavior as a way to control the director or to protect the self from the challenges and insights offered by the director. All of this and more can happen in a spiritual direction relationship. The responsibility for the quality of the relationship lies largely with the director. The director must monitor carefully the dynamics of the relationship, particularly its sexual dimension. It may be necessary to bring these dynamics to the attention of the directee when the relationship is being evaluated. Such regular evaluation is one of the best methods to eliminate any destructive sexual tendencies.

AUTHORITY. One final area of unfreedom that needs to be considered is the matter of authority and the directee's reactions to authority. Most people at some point in life have found those in authority to be bigger, stronger, tougher, older, or wiser than they are. The power and importance of authority figures in the life of the ordinary human being should not be underestimated.

Further, no human situation is free of authority figures. They are almost omnipresent throughout human life and experience. We find them everywhere—at home, in school, at church, at work, in the community. Therefore, how a person reacts to authority influences other aspects of human relationships. For example, it can color the directee's attitude toward the authority figure of the director. Undoubtedly, it will affect one's relationships with God since God is a primordial authority figure for most people.

People react to authority figures in several problematic ways. They either are defiant or docile. Sometimes, though, they are both. The first reaction refers to adolescent rebellion. By word, deed, response, and decision, directees let it be known that no one can tell them what to do. At some point in life they have been hurt significantly by an important authority person—a parent or sibling, a boss or teacher, an enemy or friend. They have now transferred their hurt or pain in a defensive manner to anyone who exercises any kind of authority, even those who do so gently and with real care and great concern. They assume a posture of anger and abiding rebellion against all authority. Their hurt, rage, and pain make it almost impossible to trust the very people to whom they are often most attracted. Rebellion is their only remedy for long-standing hurt feelings.

At the other extreme are people who have cultivated an exaggeratedly docile attitude to those in authority. These people have a fairly low sense of personal identity or self-esteem and compensate by the affirmation offered to them by important authority figures. They constantly negotiate with those in authority—those who can or actually do affirm them—for a personal sense of well-being and grounded identity. They seek their emotional security in the acceptance and affirmation of significant people who exercise some authority over them. They are passive and fearful to take personal initiative or responsibility for their life. They often show themselves most happy and content when carrying out orders. It is unfortunate that many such people have entered the priesthood or religious life. Both of these groups, priests and religious, have shown themselves remarkably adept at accepting and almost beatifying this immature attitude and response.

Docility is clearly the more subtle and devious of the responses, the one against which the director must be most on guard, because it can so impair the spiritual direction relationship. If a director suspects that a person beginning spiritual direction is inclined to depend on authority figures, the best approach is to be as nondirective and noninitiating as possible. The director should create no agenda. Rather the director should allow the directee to determine the program for every meeting. The director should even be discreet about offering simple suggestions or recommendations, for they may assume major significance to the directee and generally interfere with the directee's increasing freedom and personal responsibility. When faced with a directee seeking to develop self-esteem and a sense of self-identity from the approval and acceptance of an authority figure, a director must become more passive and less responsive, difficult though that may be.

Often the director, over a fairly long period of time, can empower a directee to discuss personal desires, longings, and inclinations, that is, embrace the part of the self that is richly graced and gifted and that actually "belongs" to the directee. At that point, the directee realizes that authority figures do not really validate personhood, goodness, or personal authenticity. These realities exist prior to any affirmation. Once again, quiet, patient, and persistent prayer is very helpful in accomplishing this important life task, particularly prayer that exposes Jesus as one who exercises the very different authority of compassion. Such a revelation can be immensely healing for anyone who is overly docile toward authority because of a fear of reflection or a deep personal insecurity. Helping the person to discover the compassionate side of Jesus is one of the best things that a director can do for a directee with a negative disposition to those in authority. The freedom that blossoms in the directee when this issue is resolved is truly extraordinary.

The only way to treat people who react defiantly to authority figures is with firm kindness. These directees often react in specific ways: abusive language aimed at the director; aggressive, sarcastic, or cynical reactions to directive suggestions; or significant independence even when it is clear that they are not acting in their own personal best interest. The director must have immense patience. Strong or harsh responses will inevitably undermine the quality of the relationship. During times like these the directee will emotionally identify the director with all the other authority persons who have hurt, punished, or threatened him or her. At some point, though, the director must confront the aggressive or rebellious behavior of the directee, but it must be done in a manner that does not threaten or reject the person. The confrontation must be preceded by a long history of care, trust, and esteem for the directee, so that it becomes clear that the criticism is about behavior, not about personhood. Such firm gentleness can often readjust the directee's attitude toward those who exercise authority.

These are the areas and issues of unfreedom that a director will often discover in a person who is beginning direction for the first time. Of course, they are not necessarily limited to those just beginning direction. I have tried to describe accurately the behavioral aspects of these unfreedoms and to suggest approaches that a director can utilize to assist the directee in dealing with destructive and inhibiting tendencies. These suggestions come from my own personal experience and derive from the working assumption that God wants the deepest possible personal freedom for his people. The work of the director is to collaborate with the Spirit of God and the directee in affecting personal freedom. The beginning of spiritual direction often proves to be the most appropriate time for the directee to confront and resolve these important areas of personal unfreedom.

Directees Experiencing Religious Conversion

I would like now to offer some reflections and recommendations about directees who are undergoing or have recently undergone an experience of personal conversion. This experience is not limited to any particular group or class of directees. Sometimes it is the reason why a person chooses to begin spiritual direction. Often the experience will be a new initiative of God with a person who has had a long history of spiritual direction, but who has been living in a kind of spiritual rut or limbo. Conversion often occurs as a result of a retreat experience or a time of intense or extended prayer in which the person has been significantly and clearly touched by the Spirit of God. Whatever the experiential catalyst, conversion deserves very careful attention from the director.

What is the shape, or contour, of this spiritual experience? How is it recognized by both the director and the directee? What pattern or stages of development exist? What can a director or spiritual guide do to assist a person receiving the important invitation from the life-giving Spirit of God? Finally, how do the director and directee together negotiate the experience of personal conversion?

Simply put, conversion is the point or process at which a person stops the old way of life and begins something new; it is literally a turning around to a new way of living that is initiated by the presence, unique power, and action of the Spirit of God. For the most part, conversion occurs in the person's unconscious, though surface phenomena also indicate its deeper reality. For example, a person may experience a sense of religious or spiritual awakening accompanied by a call to a more public and living expression of faith, charity, or service. Often these feelings go hand in hand with the reality of forgiveness, particularly of chronic sinfulness. A gradual realization of familiarity and oneness with God emerges. Often too the experience is marked by a renewed desire for self-surrender and an inclination to yield oneself more readily to the presence, love, and action of God, whatever that may be.

Some people who experience religious or spiritual conversion want to emphasize a certain point in their history, a time or place of conversion, but, as the person grows and develops, the details of the circumstances actually grow dimmer. Once the person is involved in the process of conversion and all its implications, he or she usually finds it difficult to remember or determine where or when the actual conversion took place. The person experiences a change in feeling and mood about oneself, about others, about the world, and about God. An interior shift occurs from disorder to harmony, from anxiety to peace, from conflict to integration, from reacting to life in old ways to responding to change in new and creative ways. Something old and chaotic is over, something new and dynamic has been born. Many directors emphasize this change, because they believe that it authenticates the validity of conversion. However, this is not necessarily so since such changes are common to every kind of conversion: the religious or psychological, the political or social, the moral or intellectual. In fact religious conversion can only be validated from what follows, that is, the new kind of life that emerges from the experience of conversion. The important question that needs to be asked by both the director and the directee is: What am I now going to do about this new reality?

Catalysts for conversion depend largely on whether the person is temperamentally active or passive, reflective or inattentive. The passive person tends to respond to a sense of sin, a feeling of depression or discouragement, a felt helplessness or estrangement from God. Active people note resistance to prayer, a rising sense of crisis in life, and an effort to move to some kind of new life along with an increasing intuition that something is amiss. For both types, the most common element indicative of religious conversion is a rising awareness of conflict that can only be resolved by a sharp break from the past. An increasing inner pressure to resolve conflict emerges in the consciousness of the directee.

On the one hand, others can and do play a significant part in the conversion experience. Often the most important catalyst for conversion is an interpersonal encounter while one is in crisis or conflict. Such an encounter explains why a directed retreat can be so powerful when one is on the threshold of true religious conversion. It is also why some very pointed remarks from the director can spark the insight needed to resolve inner tension.

On the other hand, almost all accounts of religious conversion seem to agree that other persons are secondary and subordinate to the direct intervention or interaction between the person and the Spirit of God. The directee may need someone to help him or her understand and process the conversion reality, but this helper or director is in no sense the direct catalyst for the conversion experience. In fact a significant discontinuity exists between the impact of the experience and any natural or human causes that temporally precede it. Ordinarily the depth and intensity of the conversion experience transcends any preceding cause; it is often the quality of the experience that tells both the director and directee that the Spirit of God has wonderfully and powerfully worked its magic. Director and directee stand in awe at the mysterious ways in which God has managed this extraordinary personal conversion.

What does the director do when conversion is the specific and immediate experience of the directee? How can the director collaborate with the Spirit of God who has initiated and promoted this experience? What emerges as the appropriate and creative way to deal with another who has been led by God to newness of life, to a new and vital personal appropriation of the self? Two things are helpful when directing someone who is in a conversion process under the guidance of the Holy Spirit: (1) to heighten awareness and (2) to sharpen the inner conflict when the person becomes aware that conversion has actually occurred. What do I mean by this? First, the director must consistently bring the directee back to the action of God, to an awareness that God is the *real* catalyst of the conversion experience. Conversation and dialogue with the directee should consistently focus on what God is doing in the life of the person, while remembering, of course, that God works in manifold ways—in nature, creating the temperament and personality of the person, in beauty, in worship, in relationships, and through new ideas and images. The point of this exercise of awareness is to ascertain the scope of the personal conversion and collaborate with it. In no way should the director allow the person to engage in any activity or behavior that will blur the awareness or offer escape from it.

Second, the director must focus and sharpen the inner crisis or conflict that is indicative of the conversion process. At the same time, the directee must make a decisive choice to resolve inner conflict. The directee does have personal alternatives—to continue an old life or, conversely, to choose a new way of being, relating, and living. The director should work with the directee to outline the crisis and the alternatives clearly and, by so doing, to arrive at a personal decision, to a realization that you cannot serve God and mammon. Such a procedure may heighten discomfort for the directee by increasing the level of tension and conflict that lead to decision making, but it is the best way for the director to collaborate with the spiritual process of personal conversion.

The director can accomplish these tasks in many ways. People often prefer not to discuss the conflictual state in which they find themselves. The director must gently insist that the directee return to and recognize inner conflict as the most important dimension of his or her life at the moment. Though the person may exhibit notable resistance and even some anger, the director must insist on exploring the meaning of the conversion experience. But even encouraging the person to ventilate feelings can be immensely helpful. To examine the reality of God also can significantly sharpen the crisis and inner conflict and may even culminate in a decisive resolution that galvanizes the person into action.

Many people undergoing conversion are ignorant of its deeper meaning. They need to receive information about and to appreciate the experience of others similarly touched by the Spirit of God. Scripture often is quite helpful. Given its theological sophistication, though, it is best to avoid the Gospel of John. Because many such people are relatively uninformed about the nature, meaning, value, and mystery of conversion, it is better to recommend the more simpler and direct Luke or the Acts of the Apostles.

Public worship and communal liturgy are excellent for sharpening the directee's conflict or crisis. Often the best place to process conversion is in the midst of those who have already experienced it and who are celebrating it together in public liturgy and prayerful worship. The strong communal element in worship assists anyone actively seeking a new style or direction of life. The person can learn much about self, God, and others from the dramatic, symbolic, and nonverbal events in communal liturgical celebration and worship.

A person can further explore, understand, and respond to the internal conflict by involvement in or commitment to evangelical service—washing the feet, as it were, of one's brothers and sisters. In such service the director needs to gauge well the level of involvement and the kinds of service that are appropriate to the deeper needs of the directee. The director must, however, avoid abusing the new and graced capacity for commitment and the graced generosity of the directee. Otherwise the directee will be frustrated rather than satisfied by such involvement in gospel service.

The director can help the person focus on the inner conflict by reading. For many directees books have considerable inner power and authority; they have a significant influence in forming the person. They also give the person a wonderful opportunity to reflect in privacy and leisure. Again the director should be able to suggest numerous titles of reflective or meditative reading. The director must be discerning in such recommendations, however, because some literature can be confusing and dull the personal crisis rather than aid in resolving it. The director's suggestions must accommodate the real needs of the directee.

A few other suggestions and admonitions might also be helpful. A director should at all costs avoid interference in the conversion process. The process is often very painful, for it reveals some very dark dimensions of the directee's personality and life. An overly tender-hearted director may want to relieve the pain or alleviate the distress of the directee. I cannot state strongly enough how misguided are such efforts. They dull crisis and cause the person to overlook the radical cost of conversion; they blur the elements of the decision to be made and minimize the real consequences and implications of conversion. The director's efforts to relieve the pain either slow or stop the process of internal conversion. Such efforts are irresponsible and disastrous; they defeat the very purpose of direction, which, after all, is the growth, development, and well-being of the directee.

The director must also avoid another kind of interference—attempting too narrowly to define the method, direction, or goal of the conversion experience. The director should not presume to know where God is leading the directee, for the director cannot tell God how to accomplish the divine purpose. It is impossible to hasten the process or to predict its ultimate goal. No encouragement, exhortation, or cajoling of the directee can accomplish conversion. For the director to hurry the directee along because of a need to succeed is to run the risk of defeating God as well as increasing and intensifying the sense of failure, guilt, and inadequacy that the directee may already feel.

Finally, the director must avoid any inclination to be possessive of the directee. The director must be aware of his or her own personal wish to be needed and of the covert ego-gratification experienced when the directee actually depends on the director. Often the directee needs to be alone rather than spend any considerable time with the director. The directee has a real desire for physical, emotional, and spiritual separation from others in order to be alone with God. It is a question not of isolation, but of intensified awareness of the self being challenged and confronted by the loving Spirit of God. For the director to be possessive or supportive of any kind of dependence blocks the deeper processes of personal conversion. It clearly inhibits the completion of the process initiated and guided by God. Direction that actually blocks God would, of course, be the very worst kind of spiritual direction.

Personally I prefer to look to the period after the conversion experience for the data and changes that validate the reality and depth of the conversion itself. The follow-up period develops in a fairly typical fashion as a process with three distinct movements or "moments." By speaking of such moments I refer not only to chronological time but also to a psychoreligious development that follows the experience of personal conversion. To gain some further understanding about its pattern and what I mean by psychoreligious development, I suggest that the reader survey the account of Paul's conversion in the Acts of the Apostles. The scriptural revelation illustrates and illuminates the postconversion experience.

Postconversion Experience

The postconversion experience is a transition from the extroverted to the integrative to the complacent. Immediately following the resolution of the inner conflict—the actual experience of conversion—the person is highly extroverted about the nature and giftedness of the experience. Frankly, the directee cannot talk enough about it. The experience gives birth to new zeal and much new energy for personal service to others. The person recounts the events eagerly to others—to anyone, in fact, willing to listen. A desire to celebrate the event(s) of conversion is ordinarily coupled with a joyful release and a sense of relief. The problems and crises that precipitated the conversion now seem miraculously gone. However, beneath the euphoria is an underlying fear that the intensity of the experience will pass. For this reason the person tries to recreate it and maintain it. At this point the director can be too encouraging and actually exploit the process of conversion, which can halt real growth in the directee. Similarly, the director can encourage the directee to tell and retell the event of the conversion until the person is fixated on its importance. Too much approval of extroverted sharing with others, too strong an affirmation of the zeal and generosity of the directee will stunt the person's spiritual growth and development. The director must try to maintain a delicate balance between affirmation and manipulation. During this postconversion time of extroverted fervor, the director's major and most important task is to affirm, without exploiting or manipulating, the person's experience and zealous generosity. If accomplished, the director can insure the grounded quality of the conversion experience.

A very quiet period follows the extroverted stage in which the person seems to lose religious zeal and spiritual fervor. Now the time has come for the directee to integrate him- or herself into a new and fuller life. This stage approximates the experience of Saint Paul after his personal conversion: first he gave himself to preaching—extroverted stage—and then he retired to the desert to integrate more deeply his experience. How does one typify or characterize this development? What happens to the directee in the transition from the extroverted to the integrative stage of religious conversion?

At this point, the early conflicts that led to conversion re-emerge and must be even more deeply resolved. The person starts to notice the conflicts again and worries that the fervor has been dissipated or, worse, that it is completely gone. Enthusiasm wanes or is replaced by a kind of spiritual ennui that is very disconcerting. Such reactions, it must be said, are perfectly normal. The director should communicate the normality of the situation to the directee.

Earlier problems, conflicts, and crises do indeed reappear, but the perspective is quite different now since there is a shift from the egocentric to the theocentric. The directee needs a great deal of encouragement from the director in order to generously and more peacefully integrate the full implications of personal spiritual conversion. The assistance of the director is needed to understand the experience and to design alternatives for a new, lived personal integration of these inner events. The director should not heighten the conflicts or crises. To do so would only intensify the fear or anxiety of the directee when it should be lessened and/or eliminated. The directee becomes frightened. It is similar to the fear experienced during isolation, when the crises and conflicts of conversion were still powerful and intense. Everything possible should be done to lessen these fears, so the person can turn energies into insights that will deepen and integrate the experience.

The director needs to tell the directee how to cope with the conflicts that have reemerged and with the subsequent fears and anxieties. Some people may remain in this agitated state for a long time because they have become disheartened or discouraged by the loss of intensity and excitement. Very gently and gradually, however, with the patient encouragement, tranquil support, and assistance of the director, the directee perseveres to integrate all the implications of conversion and eventually recovers personal assurance about the validity of the experience.

This deep personal assurance guarantees, as it were, the process of conversion and marks the close of the integration process. Again there is a willingness by the directee to share the experience, but not in any fanatical or obsessive manner. The story is now told through actions, life, and relationships rather than through mere words. The directee returns to a deep sense of personal peace and interior tranquility. Growth and religious development continue. Further struggle and temptation—particularly a fear of losing God—will occasionally return, but for now a sense of closeness to God and a subsequent quiet feeling of joy emerges. Where there once had been helplessness and hopelessness, now surface feelings of empowerment and hope. Problems and difficulties become much more subtle and more manageable.

The actual experience of conversion loses its importance and significance for the directee, because the directee can now recognize that God is working in his or her life—that God is taking active initiatives in the various dimensions of life. The experience of the present is more important and intriguing than borrowing from the past. The person can truthfully look forward to new growth and development—to the present and the future.

This rather brief description and explanation of the conversion process and the kind of growth and development that follows a true religious conversion is meant to be an aid to directors who might be called upon or invited to work with a person involved in such a graced process. Remember, though, that conversion is a complex experience with many moral, emotional, political, religious, and intellectual dimensions. The depth and power of conversion will be greatly enhanced if it is grounded in an experience of the living God and comprises a sense of intellectual truth, moral goodness, and motivational affect.

Directees Experiencing Aridity in Prayer

I would now like to offer some remarks about directees who are experiencing dryness or aridity in personal prayer. For a rather large number of people, aridity is the norm in their ordinary prayer life. More likely than not, a director will see this type of directee the most often in spiritual direction. Therefore, it is incumbent on the director to be aware of such aridity and to know how to guide, support, and encourage directees for whom dryness and aridity characterize ordinary prayer.

How can one define aridity in prayer, and what is its meaning for the directee? What can the director and directee achieve in the midst of such dry prayer? How can both be cooperative and collaborative with the action and direction of God? It is important to attend to the self-revelation and self-description of the directee, especially when the directee strongly intimates that "nothing is happening in prayer," that is, that no experience of affective consolation occurs. The person may be praying regularly, and active charity may be a regular part of his or her life. In prayer, though, few or no images appear, little affective movement, no feeling of lightness or consolation from God or others, no insights, no sense of God's active presence, and no satisfaction in or from prayer.

This thumbnail sketch is rather typical of the prayer life of so many good and generous people who also have regular spiritual direction. What can the director do when companioning such people? When a directee's prayer is characterized by aridity, the most helpful thing to do is to encourage the person to focus attention away from prayer and concentrate on life itself. Encourage the person to observe the livelier sense of God in the larger fabric of life, for God's presence can generally be found in work, leisure, nature, and relationships. Prayer does not change, but a newfound amazement and delight in all the other ways in which God enters the person's actual lived experience arises. In the midst of aridity and dryness, the person is being called to new forms of prayer, a new stage of intimacy and familiarity in the relationship with God. The dryness may actually mark the beginning of a more genuine gift of prayer, in which one is invited to find the God of consolation in the midst of personal aridity. No exercise of piety, no method of prayer, no spiritual process, no other person can bring one into a vital contact with the living God. Much patience and especially good humor is needed, for something very important is going on—a passage from meditative and discursive prayer to a more mysterious dark contemplation. Such aridity often signals the transition from active to passive prayer and into what are called nondiscursive forms of prayer.

John of the Cross notes three important realities concerning dark contemplation. First, he makes clear that discursive prayer can become factually impossible. No thoughts, words, concepts, or conceptual images occur to the person. Nor in this kind of meditative, cognitive, or discursive prayer does the individual experience personal satisfaction. Second, the person cannot focus on any concrete object as a kind of anchor in prayer. The active imagination becomes nonfunctional or dysfunctional. However, intuition and instinct—noncognitive and nonimaginative awareness and knowledge—increases. Finally, the person feels a strong but unfulfilled desire for solitude, to pray and be alone with God, even though God, at this point, seems very distant. This desire grows despite the considerable pain and difficulty associated with dryness. The person becomes validated not by the subjective satisfaction in prayer but by the charity that applies to his or her life. Therefore, it is important for the director and the directee to examine together the quality of the person's entire life.

Thomas Merton suggests that God calls a person to the prayer of faith—a passage to nondiscursive and rather dry prayer—by an insistent and urgent seeking and desire for God, undaunted by the aridity, the obscurity, and the apparent irrational quality of the quest. Anguish in prayer and a lack of meaning about one's ordinary reality can occur, and yet the person persists in the pursuit. The directee continues to require support and encouragement and needs to focus on the reality of ordinary life in which charity flourishes and a deeper compensatory sense of the love and presence of God emerges.

Often in difficult prayer the person leans on the director and needs some additional help to persevere. The directee often presumes that the director does not understand the difficulty of the situation; sometimes too the directee presumes something is emotionally wrong. It is difficult for the directee to accept the director's affirmation, support, and assurance that nothing is wrong and that this is a time of significant gift and grace initiated by God. But it is also a trying and difficult time for some directors, because of a lurking bias that makes them feel that, if they could only find the right thing to suggest to the directee, then the situation would be resolved or, at least, alleviated.

The alleged remoteness of God is actually the sign of a deepening relationship, an invitation to take the attention off oneself. It is also another example of the perennial invitation from God to self-surrender in trust. The person is being asked simply to surrender his or her control over prayer and the development of the relationship to the mysterious God of prayer. Men find this surrender much more difficult than do women. Women enter the intuitive mode of prayer much more easily than men. Men want to try harder, do more to make something happen in prayer. They need to maintain control of prayer. Men sometimes yield to a temptation to stop praying in favor of activity or become increasingly more stylized in their prayer, that is, returning to the formal prayer of the Liturgy of the Hours.

Because of powerful temptations to provoke something other than the aridity and dryness of prayer, inner life can stagnate. Growth and development in the relationship to God can halt. Rather than engage in activity, the person must be patient and wait for God. Busywork in prayer, such as reading, music, or journaling, absolutely should be avoided. It is essential to focus on life in all its rich dimensions as the forum for the more consoling action and loving presence of God. Generally life does become fuller and richer even as prayer becomes drier. In life, God's presence is revealed with more frequency, particularly in the quality of important and ongoing personal relationships. At this point, the directee should begin to notice the revelatory quality of life and love.

What are the signs that indicate this quality in the directee's life? A new and deeper sense of trust and confidence, particularly involving relationships, emerges. The person becomes increasingly compassionate toward oneself. Competition diminishes, because the person has less need to prove something or to appear successful to others. The person is less judgmental. To forgive and seek forgiveness from others becomes increasingly easy. Personal priorities and values are reorganized. With a clearer focus on the centrality of God in one's life, other issues become less significant.

This renewed focus on God leads to a prayer marked by less self-concern or self-preoccupation. Since the directee recognizes God as the source of all life, much more praise and thanksgiving enter into prayer. A new level of gentleness develops. The person feels more comfortable with vulnerability and personal weakness and much less anxious or concerned about personal failures or shortcomings. Instead a greater awareness of personal authenticity and integrity increases as do renewed desires for honesty. The inauthentic has been shed in favor of a new and deeper personal truth.

A new capacity and a personal tolerance for the ambivalent and the ambiguous is revealed in the way the person reconciles seeming opposites—action and prayer, truth and love, waiting and doing, gentleness and strength, solitude and involvement, apostolate and community. Most important, there is a growing sense of active love and operational charity. The former "oughts" and "shoulds," the unspoken expectations of others, no longer have a strong hold on the person. Only God matters. Most of life is seen and acted on in light of the person's relationship with God. For perhaps the first time, the person realizes that indeed "life is prayer." Some may think this sounds like pious fiction. But for those people who have experienced the conversion process, it is their deepest personal truth. Both director and directee can trust this reality.

When guiding a person who is experiencing aridity and dryness in prayer, a director should avoid certain issues or topics. As mentioned earlier, the director should avoid recommending any kind of busywork, especially in the form of discursive prayer. Under this rubric I include all of the active forms of prayer, such as meditation, imaginative contemplation, or contemplation of the Gospels. Any activity where the directee is ordered to provoke or manipulate internal movement in prayer should be avoided since this activity is contrary to the passivity initiated by the Spirit of God.

The directee must also avoid any escapist behavior. Since prayer is arid and dry, the directee may feel tempted to savor the compensatory presence of God in work, leisure, or relationships to the detriment of personal recollected prayer. Earlier I recommended that a director help the directee find the compensatory presence of God in life other than or in addition to prayer. Although true, it is also true that such a search should never be at the expense of prayer. Arid prayer actually is a profound exercise of personal faith. The interior and dynamic growth of faith expands the directees' perceptions, enabling them to perceive God in other facets of lived experience. If these realities dissolve the fidelity to prayer, a gradual erosion of the capacity and ability to acknowledge, enjoy, and respond to the presence of God in the rest of one's life will also occur.

Finally, both director and directee must avoid too narrow an acceptance of the reality of prayer. Prayer must be maintained, even though it may be very arid and dry. Active and discursive prayers should be avoided, because they are counter-productive or regressive for the person. Within these operational parameters, the director and directee can explore more deeply a variety of styles and forms of passive prayer. The director should not promote any interior movement or attempt to end experiential aridity. Rather the director should help the directee discover other and more appropriate ways to be present and responsive to God in prayer. It involves a subtle and delicate balancing act. More likely than not the directee will have to discover the process by individual trial and error, which obviously is a matter of personal spiritual discernment.

Directees Who Are Contemplatives

Another group of directees with special needs in spiritual direction are the men and women who are living a communal contemplative lifestyle. These men or women live in community and follow a life of solitude and withdrawal for the specific purpose of cultivating contemplative familiarity with God. I speak here of people who by nature, grace, temperament, and vocation are specially equipped to arrive in a more substantial manner at familiarity and union with God, which is the object of all spiritual direction. They form an important group in the Christian community since they focus their conscious life on their personal relationship with God. All else has been sacrificed to pursue this particular purpose. They have adapted communal living arrangements and practices in order to foster their relationship with God. They do this primarily through solitude, worship, silence, personal asceticism, and maintaining a rhythm of work and prayer.

From conversations with both contemplatives themselves and with men and women who regularly direct contemplatives,

I have discovered two areas in which contemplatives require specific directional needs. First, there can be an attempt to escape into a kind of communal legalism that restricts free choice. People seek salvation and familiarity with God in a relationship that idealizes the constitutions or rules of the community. This arrangement is a way to avoid the lived implications of true personal freedom before the living God. Directors need to help contemplatives avoid such an arrangement. They can do this by enhancing personal freedom in a communal setting. I do not advocate any kind of "anti-law" behavior. On the contrary, I support reverence and adherence to law and custom within the religious community, unless or until this behavior becomes a form of escape from the freedom that is presupposed in the honest quest for personal familiarity with God. The inclination to adopt communal legalism seems to be prevalent among contemplative men and women. Anyone called upon to direct contemplatives should be aware of this tendency and work with the person to discover and maintain a prudent and graced balance between moral law and personal freedom.

Second, spiritual directors should also be aware of a contemplative's particular needs when dealing with sexual matters and issues of affectivity. Clearly these issues are for anyone who struggles to find God in enfleshed human experience and relationships. The close-knit and cloistered quality of the contemplative community, however, often make these issues more difficult to resolve. Further, an insidious strain of either neo-Platonism or Christian stoic apathy, or both, can be at work in contemplative communities, that is, a spirituality that denies or denigrates both the body and affections. The same attitude may apply to lived charity and personal prayer. Such a spirituality allows no room for the physical or the emotional in either of these human experiences. It provokes undue problems in the quest for self-understanding and personal growth. Difficulties center around emotional rigidity, sexuality, affective relationships, and religious friendships. These difficulties become even more problematic and convoluted when associated with feelings of anxious guilt or moral integrity, particularly when the person is actually innocent before the Spirit of God.

"Roller-Coaster" Directees

Now I want to offer a few comments for what I call the "roller-coaster" type of directee. Generally this person is a member of an actively apostolic religious community. He or she is a genuinely dedicated person, often marked by considerable talents and gifts, generosity, and energy. He or she ordinarily does very well in the solitude of retreat, once settled into the more contemplative rhythm and prayer that a retreat allows, supports, and encourages. Although committed to religious values, meaning, and service, this person lacks the discipline to pray with enough consistency to cultivate a personal and meaningful relationship with God. Prayer becomes like a pendulum or roller coaster that moves from extreme to extreme, up and down, back and forth, round and round.

The individual often moves from retreat to retreat or subsists solely on irregular days of recollection. Retreat time is viewed optimistically as an opportunity to "recharge the spiritual batteries." During the intervening period between retreats or days of recollection the spiritual energy and focus that has been stored is gradually dissipated. Some emotional fervor and resolutions still exist, but seldom is it adequate to insure quiet growthful prayer between moments. Attitude to prayer as a meaningful relationship to God tends to be all-or-nothing. Life and ministry are marked by a series of sporadic outbursts of intense and even exhausting prayer, followed by virtually no attention to the personal relationship with God. Apostolic work and service are done with genuine competence, energy, faith motivation, and goodwill, but an actively cultivated relationship with God receives, at best, minimal commitment.

Many talented apostolic religious and dedicated laity face these and similar situations that frequently evoke feelings of guilt and anxiety. Usually the person possesses real insight into the situation but lacks the ascetic discipline or courage to fix it. Instead, they allow prayer to languish.

What should a spiritual director do under such circumstances? How can a director assist directees in their relationship with the God of life and love? The director must help the person resolve the all-or-nothing mentality that afflicts the personal engagement and relationship with God. In many cases, such an attitude reflects the dark side of an exaggerated idealism or perfectionism that cannot settle for less than the ideal or the perfect. Their idealism is punitive rather than redemptive; it constricts rather than liberates. Directees know what an ideal relationship with God is like and how it is personally experienced. They also know full well that, in some sense, they are incapable of such a relationship. Since a perfect relationship is not possible, they choose—with some anxiety and guilt—not to have any ongoing relationship with God in prayer.

The director must tell the directee what *is* possible, what the person can do now, no matter how distant from the ideal or the perfect. It may be necessary for the director to become a bit more aggressive, possibly for a protracted period. The director should demand some accountability from the directee. The director needs to know what the directee can do in prayer. This is not the time for the director to remain compassionate, empathetic, understanding, or supportive. In such settings, directors often support and encourage behavior that is usually debilitating and destructive to the spiritual well-being of the directee. Nor is it the time to legitimize the all-or-nothing mentality by neglecting to invite, challenge, or hold the directee accountable for the commitment to God in personal prayer. Challenge and accountability are extremely important if the relationship with God is to grow and flourish.

The directee may need further instruction in alternate methods or forms of personal prayer. Quite often the directee turns to styles of prayer of one's youth only to discover that these styles are no longer growthful, helpful, or even appropriate to mature religious experience. Unfortunately, the person has no other option, and so once again an all-or-nothing reaction to prayer occurs. Old habits have been a normal part of the person's actual experience of prayer. Once the ideal, they have now become unsatisfactory. The person can be helped immensely by being introduced to new and creative styles and methods of personal prayer. Further, the director must encourage and support the person in this process of learning until he or she is able to master a new way of praying that better and more fruitfully fits personal temperament and personal need.

Finally, the director can help the person to become more aware of the signs of God's presence and love that occur in the larger context of life, which can help the person realize that an abiding prayerful dimension exists. By no means is this meant to be a substitute for prayer, but rather to make the person aware of the faith-filled, hopeful, and loving response to God that already can be found in the richness of individual life. Such people often experience profound discouragement about their relationship to God. As they become more aware of God's loving invitations and their authentic, lived responses, their discouragement and sadness dissipates and is replaced by a more hopeful and buoyant attitude that can often generate a disciplined, renewed, and positive commitment to personal prayer.

At all costs a director must remember to never pester directees about their prayer life. Challenging and supporting someone are always creative and positive possibilities. Nagging, on the other hand, makes direction an odious ordeal by exacerbating any anxiety or guilt that the person already feels. It makes prayer demanding and difficult instead of consoling and liberating. It turns the director into a harsh taskmaster, a dictator, and severely constricts and complicates the directee's trusting relationship to the director. For all these reasons, nagging is to be steadfastly avoided.

Conclusion

These directees represent a variety of types with specific and particular needs. Any director who does direction over a fairly long period of time will eventually meet most of them. I have carefully tried to describe each group as specifically as possible. I have also tried to present from personal experience the particular reactions that a director is called upon to provide in each situation. I hope, of course, that both the description of directee type and the simple and practical suggestions and recommendations will be helpful for other directors in their work and, through them, for the many directees who seek their guidance, direction, and support. Having reflected on these various types of directees and their particular needs, let us now turn to two other topics of immense importance in spiritual direction: prayer and spiritual discernment.

Further Reading

Leonard Cranmer, *Up from Depression* (New York: Simon and Schuster, 1969).

Donald Gelpi, S.J., "The Converting Jesuit," *Studies in the Spirituality of Jesuits* 18, no. 1 (January 1986).

Thomas H. Green, S.J., *When the Well Runs Dry* (Notre Dame, Ind.: Ave Maria Press, 1979).

———, *Drinking from a Dry Well* (Notre Dame, Ind.: Ave Maria Press, 1991).

Lewis R. Rambo, *Understanding Religious Conversion* (New Haven, Conn.: Yale University Press, 1993).

3

Prayer and Spiritual Discernment

Two realities form the heart of spiritual direction: prayer and spiritual discernment. I have already mentioned a variety of perspectives about both in the preceding chapters. I now would like to systematize my reflections. I will begin with some brief remarks about the mystery of prayer and then turn my attention to more detailed thoughts about spiritual discernment and the role of personal prayer in discernment. These reflections will center both on discernment in the director and in the directee for what, I hope, are very obvious reasons.

The Mystery of Prayer

Many of the definitions and descriptions of prayer currently making the rounds in the Christian community and in the literature on spiritual direction make one very serious mistake: they describe or define prayer essentially in terms of personal activity. That is, they place the reality, the value, and the initiative for prayer with the person praying. This misconception has, I believe, very important consequences for the individual and for the development and growth of personal prayer. It creates the conviction that the direction, fruitfulness, growth, and development of personal prayer is necessarily related to personal effort and responsibility. Such a view can often lead to constriction in prayer; it provokes guilty feelings and gives birth to considerable tension and anxiety. Unfortunately, this interpretation has been around for a while; it has been passed on, blessed, and sanctioned by a long ascetical tradition within the Christian community.

A far better way to describe personal prayer is to begin with a different perspective: God as the center and starting point of prayer. Only after prayer is accepted as the action and activity of God is the response of the directee taken into consideration. In other words, prayer is God revealing divine reality to the person and, in that same revelatory action, shedding light on the mysterious reality of the person praying. It is the apt and appropriate human response to the mysterious revelation of the Spirit of God.

This definition places the initiative in the action of God. It forms the experiential basis for my assumption that God is knowable, that God has and does continue to reveal divine mystery to the human community and to the individual. Revelation occurs because God loves us very much and wants to share with us the precious riches of divine mystery. God, in his infinite imagination and creativity, makes real this divine desire to reveal, communicate, and share divine presence, mystery, and love with the person who is praying.

Further, defining prayer in such a way makes clear that the self-revelation of God leads the individual to a deeper knowledge of self. God's light illuminates the person, revealing new and startling dimensions of the personality to the person praying. Divine light enhances self-awareness and deepens self-acceptance and self-esteem. Personal truth is communicated in such a way that one sees more clearly and accepts more deeply the mysterious reality of the self in all its weaknesses and strengths. The movement of God and the person praying is mutual and reciprocal—and is the result of God's initiating activity and the presence of love in the person's life.

The derivative sense of prayer revolves around the activity of the person. That is, prayer is what the person does; it is the activity of the person. However, it is a response to the action of God, not an initiating act. The person becomes aware of and alert to the activity of God, searching for appropriate ways to respond to God's loving initiative. This responding and responsive activity is also called prayer, but in a derivative sense. It is correct to speak of what a person does as the reality of individual prayer, but only as this activity is responsive to the perceived action of God on one's life, work, and relationships.

This description of prayer allows for many styles, modes, and methods. Personal prayer is as individual and unique as the person. Each person must develop an authentic and appropriate way of responding to the living God, that is, a way of expressing his or her uniqueness to a very specific, particular, and unique manifestation of God's love and presence. The more authentic and appropriate the person's response to God's revelation, the better and more developed the person's prayer will be.

It is truly amazing how liberating this approach to prayer has been for many people. It removes a huge burden of turmoil and responsibility, guilt and anxiety. As long as people feel complete responsibility for their life of prayer, they remain paralyzed in their approach to personal prayer. However, once they see that God is the initiator of their prayer, that God cares more about their prayer than they do, that God is indeed inviting them to discover their authentic response to divine revelation, then prayer becomes more satisfying, more enlightened, and more deeply personal.

This approach to prayer has also been very helpful to me in my ministry of spiritual direction. Often I felt obligated to "teach people how to pray;" that is, how to follow the traditional understanding of prayer as primarily the activity of the one who is praying. Once I realized that prayer is God's revealing action, then I also realized that as a director my first task was to help the directee become aware of God's action in his or her life. When personal awareness and alertness to God is heightened and refined, the person quickly discovers a very personalized and unique way to respond to the action of God. This individual prayer allows for significant growth, development, and a variety of responses.

Prayer is a gift from God. It does not create God's presence or make God any more loving or available. It simply helps one to become aware of the various creative ways that God is already present and active in one's life. It consists not so much of what we do, but how much we allow God to do, to act in and through us, to "gift" us. In short, prayer is an awareness of God's constant and loving presence and action. Using this definition, prayer can appear to be very risky and powerful, a mysterious challenge that always asks us to transcend ourselves. It is a profound call and personal invitation to growth and fidelity, to transformation and freedom, to becoming a new creation—that is, a new person in God. It involves giving God the power to possess us while allowing ourselves the freedom to enter more generously into his divine embrace.

Prayer has been called a radical response to life. It is a growing interaction with one's own life, an interaction that is a response, because the God of life takes the initiative and sustains the reality of the prayer relationship. During this time one is invited only to be receptive, to respond to the movements that occur in and through life. It is not merely a matter of saying prayers but rather an openness to God in every way. Prayer is God's revelation in the joys, pains, moods, and day-to-day ordinary events of life. All this and more forms the "stuff" and substance of prayer. No part of our faith life, our experience, or our vision excludes or escapes the loving presence of God.

Prayer, therefore, is not just a part of life, but *all* of life. It is not part of our thoughts, emotions, images, feelings, actions, and reactions; it is *all* of them. To pray is to think and to feel and to live constantly in response to God. One must let God be in life and experience. This does not imply that one cannot take the time to pray and be alone with God. It only means that prayer should in no way be divorced from life. Everything in one's life is part of God's constant concern for us. God is not indifferent to any part of our lives.

Sometimes a person is more alert to his or her presence with or to the living God, only to rediscover the wonderful truth of the divine presence that pervades one's entire life. This awareness, too, is prayer, and its purpose is to help us remember that God is part of everything in life. Such experience presupposes that prayer is essential to be in relationship with the living God, to realize the presence of the loving Other who is obsessed with love of us. In prayer the true self can emerge because the person is loved and accepted without condition or qualification.

With such awareness and such prayer the person can finally come to know and trust this honest and gentle, challenging and supportive God who offers unconditional love. Trust of this magnitude gently develops outside the time spent in prayer and gradually confirms the belief that, despite weakness, emptiness, and dryness, God is present and loving at all times, in all places, and in all circumstances and is working very powerfully on one's behalf. Consequently, absolute honesty with God is essential. Each of us has a unique relationship with God, so each relates in a way no one else will or can. To be less than completely candid is to waste time.

Furthermore, prayer heightens and deepens the importance of letting God love us as we are. We need not prove anything to God; we could not do so, even were it needed. We cannot coerce, negotiate, or purchase the love of God. It already exists, for *God is love*. All we need to do is to be open and available to the undeserved and unreserved love that God has for us. It makes no sense to compare one's personal prayer with the prayer of someone else. Perhaps some value may come in hearing others speak of their prayer, but we each pray as no one else does. Rather what is needed is nurturing and relishing the wonderful uniqueness of one's own gift of prayer.

To pray honestly and uniquely leads to the awareness that one cannot live without God. When we pray peacefully in response to the action of God, we come to have an almost desperate need of the Other. Like the process of falling in love, we allow God to entice us, draw us, ground us, even seduce us. Prayer invites us to a type of surrender that leads to deeper freedom: the freedom to be our richest, truest self; the freedom to love in the same measure as one has been loved. When we experience a profound sense of being totally and unconditionally loved for who we are, we are set free. We begin to know and receive true identity and personhood.

Difficulties in Prayer

We must remember, though, that prayer can be difficult. It is difficult not because of technique or focus, but because it involves new and deeper levels of trust. It is a constant struggle for us to let the loving God take over our lives and allow ourselves to diminish before the action of God in order to find deeper love and personal freedom. Yet prayer is its own remedy, for only by praying do we grow in the depth of trust and surrender that allows God to love us with all of the imperfections that mark our lives. In this process of trust and surrender lies the real and perennial difficulty of prayer.

Getting into a rut or a stylized routine in prayer becomes a serious obstacle for some people. They have lived far too long with a particular method that has become empty, tedious, or even boring. It no longer is an apt expression of oneself before God. What has happened? Generally, most people have a rather limited spectrum of behavior that they call prayer. It has taken time to learn and develop this behavior. Pray by rote has become *the* way to pray. Sometimes, though, people can change in new and significant ways, and the behavior that was called prayer no longer fits them; it no longer expresses in any authentic fashion their personal lives before God. Both the fruitless repetition and the inappropriate style or method of prayer induces tedium. When this occurs one needs to find another style of prayer, a different place to pray, or a posture or subject for prayer that will better express the new person that now appears before God.

A good spiritual director should be familiar experientially with a broad spectrum of modes and styles of prayer. For example, people who feel caught in a routine ordinarily have been using the Scriptures as their regular source of prayer for a lengthy period of time. A director might tell such directees to discontinue this practice as their ordinary response to the action and initiatives of God. Instead they could be encouraged to compose letters or create dialog as is often done in marriage encounter experiences. Or perhaps they could try some free-flowing drawings of a nonpictorial, nonrepresentational style to express their interior reactions to God in their lives. Similarly, some people find comfort and consolation in a bodily response to God's revelation, such as a spontaneous dance, to express their responsiveness. Some forms of group prayer are also helpful: shared prayer, various kinds of charismatic prayer, or the so-called colloquial sharing of prayerful reflections on the word of God in Scripture.

The director can help directees expand their understanding of prayer by showing them that what had been traditionally called prayer is a narrow understanding of the reality and possibilities of personal prayer. For example, in Spain during the time of Saint Teresa of Avila, a prevalent notion reduced prayer strictly to mental activity—the prayer of meditation. Vocal prayer was not "worthy" of the name. We might compare the Spanish attitude toward vocal prayer with the kind of superficial relationships we often have with casual acquaintances, the kind of relationships that lack any variety or real interpersonal involvement. People react the same way in prayer and in their relationship with God. They allow an unidimensional and tedious style to develop because they do not know any other way to relate to God. Once they develop other relational styles and skills, the boredom usually ends.

A second difficulty in prayer centers around an exaggerated preoccupation with the self. The person becomes so preoccupied that he or she cannot focus on the action of God in life. Often the source of this difficulty is a long-term sense of personal inadequacy, which leads one to focus primarily inward. A lowered self-esteem, a sense of personal deficiency, and even some depressive tendencies are common traits. Prayer is anxiety-ridden and often very difficult and painful, because the person is concerned about "doing it right." Every prayerful thought or spiritual movement reminds the person of personal limitations and imperfections. Ordinarily one cannot continue prayer that leaves one's sense of self so eroded. Consequently, some directees simply discontinue. A rudimentary desire to pray certainly remains, but it is usually reduced to some type of formalized prayer, such as the recitation of the Psalms or the Rosary.

Frankly, preoccupation with the self is among the most troublesome of the "ordinary" difficulties that can occur in prayer. It demands from the director utmost patience and skill that will enable the directee to discover, accept, and come to a clearer realization of God's unconditional and unqualified love. The task of the director is to facilitate this realization. Only then can the person be freed from intense, debilitating, and relentlessly negative self-preoccupation. Often such people are neurotically scrupulous, marked by a sense of personal guilt, unclear mental perceptions, and very low self-esteem. For a time the director may need to become the working conscience for the directee, while a new image of God slowly develops and a new and more mature moral sense awakens.

A further difficulty occurs in prayer when people exert too much personal effort trying to make the prayer "successful," a rather self-righteous approach to prayer predicated on the understanding that prayer is something one does and that, if one does it intensely enough, then God *must* respond. A simple imaginative exercise can often help. How does a flower blossom?, a director may ask. When a directee answers that a flower blossoms by receiving sun and rain, then transfer of the imaginative insight to prayer is possible. In other words, the directee needs to realize that prayer is not something that one does, but rather is something that is done to one. Again, it is the convinced realization that prayer is the act of God revealing divine mystery to an individual. Thus, the individual needs to experience prayer as a gift in order to be free enough to receive the gift of God's love.

Such persons often feel tense and manifest this tension in physical rigidity. The director can suggest some physical relaxation exercises or recommend more relaxed forms of prayer, such as nature walks, the use of religious music as a catalyst for prayer, natural or artistic beauty as a source of prayerful contemplation, or ordinary breathing exercises. It may require some patience on the director's part since people tend to resist suggestions that may not necessarily fit their narrow conception of prayer. They believe that prayer *should* be difficult and intense; that it *should* be dependent on their effort and labor. Since physical relaxation exercises are neither intense nor difficult, directees do not take them seriously. For this reason, directors must gently but firmly remind directees that relaxation exercises may eventually liberate them from debilitating personal experiences.

Relying on nostalgic memories of prayer can also be serious. People who have this problem fixate on the past. Certainly experiences of God in prayer are precious memories, especially experiences that served as catalysts for important personal growth, insight, or decision making. We all need to recollect the past so that we can look to the future with hope and confidence. Sometimes, though, looking back can become a form of imprisonment. For example, many people who keep a journal from previous retreats frequently refer back to them when renewing their current experience of and with God. Reviewing one's journals is important, but it is also possible to fixate on them in such a way that limits or inhibits further growth in faith and prayer. Instead of going back, it may actually be more worthwhile to move on in prayer. Often this period is referred to as *kairos*, a richly graced opportunity that allows the present and the future to exercise its collective magnetism. Now may be the time for the directee to hear the existential word of God.

A director may need to help directees become more existentially alert and more alive to the present as the forum in which God speaks personally relevant words of love or personal forgiveness. A growing alertness to the present will almost inevitably disclose some new dimensions of prayer, especially during times of important personal change or transition, such as a new job, a change of living situation, a geographical move. Any change in routine usually requires a new pattern of prayer. Once the director brings the present into focus, the directee's nostalgic fixation on the past is broken and new growth and development can occur. As in so many other aspects of spiritual direction, a simple awareness of and alertness to the present offers the best solution.

Exaggerated guilt also inhibits the growth and deeper development of prayer. How much help a director can offer depends on the intensity of feelings. Guilt can be related to Christian conscience, but it can also stem from the psychological reality of the superego. It is the guilt associated with the superego that inhibits growth in prayer. Psychological guilt torments with unassimilated ideals. That is, society expects a person to conform to certain behavioral and social norms, but the person is unable to assimilate or integrate these expectations. The directee recognizes the gap between proposed ideal behavior and actual performance. Inevitably, the person blames him- or herself for this inability to perform acceptably. In extreme cases, such an attitude can provoke intense and often paralyzing guilt. The directee views God and others as demanding, judgmental, and punitive parents. Consequently, it is hardly surprising that a person wracked by such feelings of guilt would find prayer an anxious and frightening experience.

The director must concentrate on values rather than ideals. Instead of acknowledging the unrealistic ideals, the directee consistently blames him- or herself. As long as the focus lies with the ideals, guilt will continue and probably become even more intense and debilitating. It is important to remember that societal ideals are wholly extrinsic to the person. However, a person already may have internalized a set of values and may be, in fact, completely committed to them. For example, people may have demonstrated a lived commitment to fidelity in relationships, even when the relationships have become trying or difficult. They persevere in dry prayer, not simply because prayer is an obligation but because they value prayer. Deeply integrated into a personal moral code, these values have a dynamic and liberating effect. The values are realized in behavior and performance, offering a direction for the future that the directee believes is realistically attainable. The directee wants to be true to these values but remains trapped in the impossibility of unassimilated goals and ideals. A focus on value and a concentration on commitment to value will gradually liberate the directee from the tyranny of the ideal. A newfound freedom of spirit develops as the person realizes experientially the joy arising from lived commitment to personal value.

Even relatively "free" people experience some guilt regarding anger and sexuality. They feel guilt without necessarily being guilty. They must be able to recognize the difference between feelings and morality, which is a very hard lesson to learn. Yet it is one that we must all master. Feelings are essentially amoral; neither good nor bad, right nor wrong. Feelings are morally neutral. They are a spirit-body reaction or response to internal or external stimuli. It is how a person chooses to act that raises the issue of morality. What one *does* as a result of emotional reactions may be good or bad, right or wrong, but the feelings themselves are without any moral connotation. Neither praise nor blame is required for spontaneous emotional reactions that arise from stimuli over which a person has little or no control.

Once a directee learns this lesson—the nonmoral quality of emotional responses—then it is relatively easy to deal with the troublesome and often guilty feelings asociated with anger and sexuality. Once one accepts the feelings and begins to integrate them in a healthy manner and without fear, then guilt quickly dissipates. Generally, a mature attitude tends to heal the sense of separation from God that the person has experienced over guilty feelings. If a person can bring all of these feelings—anger, guilt, sexuality—to prayer and is able to let go or allow the healing powers of God to enter, then that person will actually experience liberation.

Often the source of misplaced guilt can later be seen as a wonderful sign of God's love, thus freeing one to enter more deeply into the love relationship of personal prayer.

Bringing such feelings to prayer is one simple way that a director can aid, support, and encourage people who suffer from deep-seated feelings of guilt that are not rooted in personal sin. These feelings become a graced opportunity to trust God more deeply and to surrender the guilt in prayer. The directee is then empowered to face the truth of God's love—a love that makes him or her more deeply free before God. Praying about or with such feelings can also be very helpful in other dimensions of the directee's affective life.

A final area of difficulty in prayer lies in a pattern of moral disorder or real moral fault. Here the directee is moderately or implicitly conscious of behaviors that are contrary to the love of God in his or her life. Generally, personal behavior is involved that is destructive to oneself or others. Thus, a directee experiences difficulty in prayer because some aspect of life is askew, and self-appraisal, examination, and personal scrutiny are not practiced. The major mechanisms at work here are intellectualization, denial, and rationalization. All join forces to protect the individual from harm.

Typically, in spiritual direction a directee will discuss five areas of his or her personal life in addition to reflections about personal prayer. I expect to hear about a person's physical well-being, work situation, the quality of personal relationships, decision-making skills, and the affective and emotional reaction to internal and external stimuli that mark ordinary human life. These topics can serve as a useful checklist in the course of regular spiritual direction. When I have not heard about one or another of them for a long time and there is a concomitant difficulty in prayer, I become somewhat suspicious. Generally, prayer will be marked by a sense of discomfort, a quiet kind of anxiety or desolation that is increasingly disturbing to the person. Until this personal disorder is resolved, a state of anxiety and difficulty in prayer will continue.

The major stumbling block invariably lies in the area of relationships and/or affective or emotional reactions. Two important areas can easily escape notice and detection: issues of behavioral justice and felt but unexpressed anger. I speak of justice in terms of the ways that the person consciously oppresses others and of anger in terms of felt frustration that is experienced but not creatively expressed. The directee may neglect to discuss these areas because they are problematic. People simply do not volunteer information about areas of life that are uncomfortable. Very often a person has an instinctual or intuitive sense of what is wrong but ignores it in the hope that praying will make it go away. Inevitably, prayer fails and will continue to fail until the person becomes authentically honest before God or until someone else points out the behavioral disorder and is supportive while the disorder is being eliminated with the loving help of God's Spirit. Only in this way will the difficulty in prayer be remedied.

Under such circumstances, life and prayer come together. No authentic prayer can exist unless life itself is authentic. We need not be perfect, but we must be wholly honest with ourselves, with God, and with others. Any truly moral evil in life will ordinarily impede prayer if it is not admitted personally and surrendered in prayer to God's forgiveness. The spiritual director may have to probe delicately to discover whether the directee is defending or protecting some dimension or facet of his or her life. The director even may have to identify the moral disorder. When a director suspects a pattern of disordered or sinful behavior exists, one of the best things to do is to bring the directee back to regular self-examination and the exercise of the examen of consciousness. With this kind of grace-filled and Spirit-led self-examination as an anchor, the person may be able to discover for him- or herself why prayer is faring so badly.

These are some of the ordinary or "normal" difficulties that directees experience in personal prayer. I have tried briefly to describe the nature of these difficulties and some of the generally accepted aids that a director can offer to help resolve problematic dimensions of prayer. These suggestions and recommendations have proved to be helpful for most directees experiencing difficulties in personal prayer.

Further Reflections on Personal Prayer

Before moving on to the important subject of spiritual discernment, one or two further reflections concerning prayer need to be said, including a word about the subject of "legislated prayer." The purpose or motive behind legislated prayer in the canonical sense is to set aside a time for prayer for each person in the religious community or family. The intention of the rule is not so much to invoke or impose an obligation to pray, but rather to insure that time be made available for what the person deeply wants to do. In a society that is largely workaholic and likes to produce results, the intention is to assure that apostolic or ministerial functions do not become overwhelming so as to eliminate the time that a person actually wants to devote to personal prayer.

Unfortunately, too few religious men and women are aware of the reason for legislated prayer. The juridical or canonical demands provoke anxiety and guilt rather than a sense of gratitude for the encouragement and opportunity to pray. Consistently, the director will have to remind the directee of the true intent of the rule. The director must gently unburden the person from the sense of obligation that often surrounds and inhibits prayer. Any coercion can seriously disrupt mature growth and development in prayer. To "force" someone to pray is like telling people that they must kiss their spouses at the end of the day. If a couple exchanges marital intimacies merely out of compulsion or obligation, clearly their marriage is either dead or dying. So too with prayer. Thus, it is extremely important to support and encourage prayer that does not depend for its existence on law or any kind of juridical obligation.

At best, prayer is always a matter of purity of intention by which every aspect and dimension of life is continually and consciously being redirected toward the living God. It is the normal and ordinary response to the realization of God's gifts to the person. As this realization and awareness grows and takes hold of one's consciousness—that God is gracious and constant in gift-giving—the directee will pray more maturely and more responsibly, with considerable devotion, personal satisfaction, and spiritual consolation.

The general process of growth in prayer moves along a continuum from active to passive, complex to simple, cognitive to imaginative, intellectual to affective, self-directed activity to passive acceptance of spiritual gifts. This shift in the rhythms and processes of prayer accompanies the deepening of prayer that marks the presence of the living spirit of God. Both director and directee can use these criteria to evaluate the actual development and growth of the directee's prayer.

Spiritual Discernment

Spiritual discernment is a very large topic about which much important and serious literature has been written. It is at the very heart of faith, growth, development, and meaningful spiritual direction. Discernment is perhaps the most important aspect of the director and directee relationship. It provides the ongoing dynamism for spiritual direction as both parties work together to discover, illuminate, and understand the rich experience of the directee.

Discernment is understood in a variety of ways and in a variety of devotional contexts. In the current literature on the subject, two distinct but overlapping meanings emerge. In one theological context discernment is used to describe a process that leads to clarity about God's will for the individual. Although of considerable theoretical and practical import, it is not the focus of these reflections. For the purposes of this work, I wish to limit my understanding of discernment to the personal process by which an individual comes to understand, interpret, and act upon the authentic movements of the Spirit of God in his or her personal experience.

In the introduction to this work, I referred to George Bernard Shaw's interpretation of Saint Joan of Arc's discernment experience. Most people who ponder Joan's rhetorical reply ("Doesn't everyone?") when asked whether she hears voices are deeply touched by its personal truth. Everyone concerned about the purpose, meaning, and direction of their lives knows exactly what she means; it reflects their own understanding of life. To understand the source, to interpret the meaning, to do the bidding of such authentic and divine promptings is really my definition of spiritual discernment.

Everyone who seeks meaning in life must learn to listen with all their capability in order to recognize the single voice that bears a thousand names. It is the voice spoken to us from the center of our personal being. It brings to each individual an intuition, a sense, an understanding of the unchanging meaning, value, and oneness of life. It speaks to us through word, image, or experience; looking or listening are ultimately one experience when we have ears to hear and eyes to see.

The process of discernment is the task of testing the various spirits, or voices, by expressing them, recreating them (perhaps in an audible or visible form of our own), and certainly by realizing their meaning in our lives. For the most part, our efforts will seem woefully inadequate. We will fall again and again. We will experience pride and inertia, false starts and even failures, but it is the perseverance itself that will sharpen our hearing.

Recent years have witnessed the growing power of the human person over nature. We seek to control everything from the smallest atom to the largest universe. Unfortunately, with the newfound control has come a parallel loss of the interior world of meaning and value. Nevertheless, by divine grace many people are being driven to search again for meaning in life, for value and depth and purpose in personal experience. Clear signs point to a rebirth, a renaissance, of this quest for the Spirit of God, this longing for the experience of God's Spirit within.

Testing the spirits is what I mean by discernment in the relationship of spiritual direction. It is the process by which one comes to an interior clarity about the source of personal experience. The directee arrives at a deeper understanding of the meaning, direction, and pattern of the experience, and, finally, is empowered with the energy and courage to do the bidding of the Spirit of God with increased confidence and joy. Though this process has many facets, it is open and available to all people of goodwill who are desirous of a deeper faith relationship with the living God.

The Process of Spiritual Discernment

Let me now reflect on some of the practical dimensions of spiritual discernment. I will begin with a few remarks based on my own personal experience. Here I draw from examining discernment about my own life and conducting spiritual direction for others, in which discernment is an essential and integral part.

Both the long tradition of teaching about discernment and my own personal experience tell me that there is no "canonized" way to conduct spiritual discernment. Sacred Scripture itself points to a variety of techniques, methods, or processes by which a person or community comes to understand the source, direction, purpose, and meaning of experience. Dreams, lived parables, prophetic utterances, success in life, casting of lots, and interior personal reactions of peace and joy in biblical literature either indicate, illuminate, or explain the actions of God in individual or communal experience. All these realities are used by God in the biblical narratives to reveal divine presence and invitation to the person or community.

Although helpful techniques or methods in spiritual discernment do exist neither ultimately guarantees real success. To explain or expect success we must look toward other realities: (1) the antecedent and unqualified love of God for the person or community and (2) the personal disposition of the individual. First, God's unqualified and unconditional love guarantees divine revelation to each of us. God's Spirit works within each person to validate and perhaps even guarantee that the person can and will arrive at a competent understanding and interpretation of individual personal experience. Second, the predispositions of the person are far more important and influential than any technique or method for spiritual discernment. These predispositions vary but have aspects in common. Common points illuminate the antecedent dispositions that are most needed for successful spiritual discernment.

The central disposition for discernment is trustful surrender—trust in the love, the promises, the fidelity, and the providential care of God—to the initiatives and actions of God. This disposition is clearly and aptly exemplified at the end of the first chapter of the Acts of the Apostles. The Apostles are intent on choosing a successor for Judas, an important decision for this young community of the risen Lord. The communal prayer led by Peter demonstrates their corporate and individual dispositions. It is a profound statement of their trust, hope, and confidence in God's promises to care for the fledgling community. They believe that the enterprise belongs wholly and entirely to God and display a rare confidence that a loving and active God will act in the community's best interests.

The new community employs a technique or method that may strike the modern reader as either primitive or superstitious, irrational or dumb. Although the decision is immensely important to the community, it is resolved by casting lots, that is, by pure chance. It is not the power or rationality of the method or technique, but rather dispositions of trust and confidence in the caring presence of the living God that guarantees the success of their discernment. Such trust and freedom of spirit epitomizes the personal dispositions that are necessary for accurate, fruitful, and successful spiritual discernment. Thus, the process of discernment is informed and animated by the profound trust of the group.

It is important to note, however, that, though one may arrive at a very high level of certitude about the action of God in one's life, such an attitude is not infallible. Spiritual discernment is changeable; new experiential data, new life experience, new relationships, or new information may illuminate or clarify the source, meaning, or direction of one's life, all of which form the existential word of God. Such variety, of course, implies an alertness to and an awareness of personal experience and the increasingly refined ability to distinguish the voice of God from other voices that speak to one's consciousness.

Further, though no particular technique or process is essential or, for that matter, foolproof, some experiential realities are clearly implied in the personal predispositions of the directee. One cannot do discernment without a regular rhythm or pattern of personal prayer, self-reflection, self-awareness, and self-examination. Personal prayer gradually, gently, and inexorably hones and refines the interior sensibility and sensitivity to the word of God. Both self-reflection and self-awareness make one aware of the multifaceted and shifting reality of personal experience. Self-examination allows one to sift through interior experiences in order to ascertain their origin, meaning, direction, and purpose, leading to the purity of heart that creates trust and surrender to God. Rhythm and balance are the real prerequisites for serious and successful spiritual discernment. Discernment without a pattern of personal prayer is misguided; discernment and prayer without reflection and awareness is vacuous!

Furthermore, all of the foregoing implies that decision-making discernment, that is, seeking the will of God, is extraordinarily difficult when isolated from an ongoing lived pattern of personal prayer, reflection, and self-examination.

In such a case the antecedent sensibility to the presence and reality of God will be clearly lacking. The person will be generally inattentive to the actual presence of God and will, more likely than not, engage in self-seeking rather than God-seeking activities.

I mention this last point because of its practical implications for the ministry of spiritual direction. Often a person seeks spiritual direction when an important decision has to be made. A directee may have a desire to seek God, but is notably lacking in the resources or dispositions to do so. The person is looking for a magic confirmation of the decision that already has been made. Since the person lacks any rhythm of prayer or reflection in life, he or she is incapable of the enlightened spiritual discernment that is being sought. In such cases, the director best serves the interests of the directee by encouraging a delay in decision making until a regular pattern of prayer, self-examination, and self-reflection is established. No particular technique or strategy of discernment needs to be stressed, but patterns do provide the resources and personal tools that are necessary.

What, then, is helpful for both the director and directee in understanding the various spiritual movements they both experience? What data and phenomena should both address in attempting to understand and respond to the authentic work of God? What is of practical use to them? How can the director help a directee become a more discerning person?

Two things are helpful for the director when assisting others in the process of spiritual discernment. First, it is important for the director to garner as accurate an understanding as possible of the spirit of the directee since the director will be interpreting the directee's religious experiences and spiritual movements. Second, the director must attend to his or her own religious experience, a prime resource when listening to the religious experience of the directee.

The director must determine the religious spirit or temperament of the directee. Such an assessment is a very simple way to express the first principle of spiritual discernment:

similar spirits provoke interior harmony; dissimilar spirits induce inner discord. The Spirit of light and goodness—God's own Spirit—provokes light, goodness, and peace in a similar human spirit while this same Spirit of God generates discord or lack of harmony in a disordered human spirit. The opposite is also true, that is, disorder elicits discord in an enlightened or well-ordered human being but provokes harmony in a person who is disordered. This principle has been borne out over and over again in the Christian tradition.

What should the director be aware of when faced with such an assessment? Do particular character traits indicate the directee's personality? What signs are important in this provisional assessment of the directee? In other words, how does the director conduct a preliminary discernment?

Signs of a "Good-Spirited" Directee

Ostensibly, determining a directee's spirit should be cut and dried; however, the practical implementation is much more subtle and sophisticated. Theoretically, a directee who is growing in personal responsibility, personal freedom, and personal maturity, who is developing Christian virtue—particularly the theological virtues of faith, hope, and charity—is a person of good spirit. On the other hand, the person who is becoming more vicious in behavior, disposition, or temperament is a person of dark spirit. Theoretical answers presuppose, of course, that such distinctions are neat and clear. It presumes the director is able to make a definitive assessment of the directee's spirit, temperament, and disposition. In actual practice, this does not often happen.

More likely the directee's life is a complicated mix of generous and virtuous moments with significant episodes of incredible darkness and disorder. Paul in his letter to the Romans describes his dual nature: "I cannot understand my own behavior. I fail to carry out the things I want to do, and I find myself doing the very things I hate . . . for though the will to do what is good is in me, the performance is not, with the result that instead of doing the things I want to do, I carry out the sinful things I do not want." Most directors and directees can see themselves in Paul. What should a director be aware of in order to help assess the spirit or temperament of the directee? What are the operational signs of a person of "good spirit"? a person of "dark spirit"?

Because of the subtlety and ambiguity of the human heart, these questions are difficult to answer. They lie, however, at the very core of spiritual direction. Since it is so difficult (perhaps impossible) to estimate, evaluate, or judge the actual lived faith, hope, and charity of another, the director's assessment of the directee's "spirit" will also entail much difficulty and ambiguity. Dispositional and behavioral indicators do exist, though. These signs can help a director arrive at an accurate assessment.

The most important signs of a "good spirit"—that is, a person in whom the action of the Spirit of God is marked by spiritual peace and harmony—appear in no particular priority. The person generally exhibits a notable reverence for life, which is very much in keeping with the biblical revelation of a God who also reveres life. Such commitment is necessary if one wants to become a person of discerning heart. The great commandment of God throughout the Scriptures is always about life, "There are two ways that are open to you, a way to life and a way to death. Choose life." The Scriptures further tell us that our God is a God of the living, not of the dead. In Jesus' great revelation about his own mission, he simply notes that he has come so that we may have life in abundance. A good-spirited directee, then, ordinarily exhibits an enthusiasm about being alive and exudes a clear sense of devotion to life in all its manifestations: physical, emotional, relational, intellectual, imaginative, spiritual, professional, and ministerial. A good directee values breadth of life and life-experience and attempts to understand and assimilate this experience. All of these traits come together as nurturing behavior, so that life may grow more vivid and more vibrant. The directee manifests intellectual curiosity and alertness, attention to intimacy and friendship, concern about prayer and reflection, and dedication to improving professional and ministerial skills.

What are the practical implications of this dedication to life? If one has not read a book in the last ten years, if one is afraid of the intellectual life, if new ideas are threatening, then one is not alive. Therefore, it is doubtful that such a person would be open to God, since God cannot come in truth to anyone who has chosen to shut down the life of the mind, the very place and reality where truth is available. Hope is a divine gift. Dreams and visions generate the freshest kind of hope. If one's imagination is dead, if one is afraid to dream—to have visions, if you will—God cannot come in hope. If one's emotional life is moribund, if one is afraid of emotions because they make life and relationships difficult, if one avoids anger or joy or sexual feelings and has chosen to repress the entire affective area of life, then one cannot know the consolation of God, because to do so is an emotional experience. To discern the designs of God without knowing consolation is virtually impossible. If one has few or no meaningful relationships, if one stands in fear of people, if one is socially or relationally withdrawn, then one cannot know God in charity. The person is truly devoid of life. Thus, one has to stay alive at all costs because our God is the God of the living.

This description of a good-spirited person may seem to be an idealized portrait of someone who is merely curious about a humane life without much interest in pursuing faith realities. On the contrary, a good-spirited person seeks spiritual direction because of a sense of mystery about life, an intuition of the numinous that invites us to experience a deeper life. Reverential regard for life is a response to divine invitations.

Yet good-spirited persons experience the ordinary shocks, disappointments, embarrassments, and failures of the human situation. However, they meet them with courage and spiritual energy. These two qualities form a second set of signs or indicators that the person is of good spirit.

People of good spirit exhibit an energy and vigor even in the face of personal difficulties in life. This energy is displayed in numerous life settings: loving fidelity in relationships with difficult people who try one's patience and compassion; personal integrity in a society and culture that seems to devalue trust and personal truth; competence and commitment to professional duties and personal obligations even at the cost of personal convenience or comfort; perseverance in prayer that is dry, dark, or subjectively dissatisfying; honest confrontation of one's own personal biases and prejudices, such as racism, sexism, and homophobia. These experiences demand dynamic fortitude to act in ways that protect, nurture, and encourage the personal life of faith, hope, and charity and, at the same time, resist whatever threatens, impedes, or destroys that life.

A truthful clarity of vision about self, God, others, and the world is another sign of good-spirited people. Their faith perceptions are notably accurate and objectively verified. Grace and gift are seen for what they really are; sin and darkness are acknowledged without undue embarrassment or guilt. Good-spirited people perceive, assimilate, and judge reality with a sense of balance. The time frame of a person's life is seen without distortion: there is no fearful fixation on the past or anxious anticipation of the future. The present is accepted and valued as the only time of grace and gift.

The overt signs of truthful clarity are manifold in the person's life and experience. They include

1. an honest and reverential approach to God, because God is Creator and Lord, Friend and Companion, Father and Mother;

2. an honest self-presentation to others, so that there is a quality of authenticity and appropriateness

about personal relationships—a "what-you-see-is-what-you-get" transparency—that is deeply attractive to others;

3. a gracious acceptance and tolerance of others without denying their actual liabilities or failures;

4. a similar tolerance and acceptance of oneself;

5. a sensibility to the grandeur of God and the grace-filled reality of the world;

6. a desire to help make the world a more just and peaceful locale for all of God's people.

These are just some of the many dispositional and behavioral signs of a person whose life and spirit are turned toward God, a spirit attuned to and in harmony with the Spirit of God.

Finally, I have noted in directees of good spirit a quality of patient and even optimistic tolerance for the ambiguities of life, the result, I believe, of a deep faith and trust in the loving action of God. Such a worldview operates from the conviction that God is Lord of our history and that, in the words of Julian of Norwich, "all will be well, all manner of things will be well." Good-spirited people appreciate the inherent ambiguity of human experience. Experience has taught them that things are not merely black or white or even gray. Rather life is in technicolor. They understand that it is difficult to follow the various strands of experience or to interpret the meaning of the fabric of life with any notable clarity. They have patience with the activity of God and a deep conviction that God will indeed clarify meaning and direction in good time. The fruit of such patience and tolerance for ambiguity is a deeper quality of peace within the person.

Good-spirited people manifest a sense of balance and personal security in their behavior; they appear to be in control of the direction of their lives. They can do this not because they are actually in control but because their faith and trust in God has given them an inner-grounded conviction that life does have direction and purpose and that God is working it all out in the midst of much ambiguity, ambivalence, and seeming lack of clarity. Experience has proven this for them, and it is this experience that grounds their convictions about God.

To reiterate, I generally turn to the following signs when making a judgment or personal assessment about the spirit of a directee: genuine reverence for life, courage and spiritual energy, honest and integral clarity of vision, and patient and optimistic tolerance for the ambiguities and ambivalences of life. Some combination of these qualities indicates the person's congruence with the Spirit of God and allows me more accurately to understand and interpret the various interior spiritual movements of the person.

These indicators will often show themselves in a notable compassion for self and others and a willingness to forgive and seek forgiveness when appropriate. Both of these external manifestations—compassion and forgiveness—serve as behavioral signs of the work of the Spirit in a good-spirited person. They guarantee or validate a Godward direction initiated by the Spirit of God.

I need to offer a disclaimer at this point, lest I frighten too many directors and/or directees. In some sense I have idealized the directee of good spirit. I have done so only for the sake of clarity and emphasis. Few directees will actually have all the qualities that I have described; the few who do will seldom have them to the same degree. Many directees, however, have some or all of these qualities or characteristics, which is more than enough, I think, to qualify them as persons of good spirit.

Religious Movements in the Director

In addition to the attention given to the spirit of the directee, the director must also attend to individual interior movements during spiritual direction. Awareness and attention to one's personal interior movements are among the most important tools or resources available to the director in spiritual direction and spiritual discernment.

Every spiritual director brings his or her history, temperament, and experience of God—his or her own spirit—to the spiritual direction conversation. They serve as the filter through which the director hears the experience of the directee. Ordinarily the directee's experiences serve as stimuli or catalysts for the director; they provoke new interior experiences—thoughts, images, intuitions, feelings, judgments. The director must train him- or herself to pay attention to these movements. What kind of interior movements are caused by the self-revelation of the directee? What effect do these movements have on the director? The answers to these questions are of utmost importance and lie at the heart of spiritual direction.

The working principle here is the gospel declaration that "where two or three meet in My name, I shall be there with them" (Mt 18:20). I am convinced that Jesus' statement applies to the inner dynamics of the spiritual direction encounter. The working assumption of spiritual direction is that director and directee have indeed gathered together in the Lord's name. When this is true and not a mere assumption, I find myself reexperiencing the Lord's presence as I attend to the self-revelation and self-communication of the directee. As I turn to my own interior movements that are provoked by the words, gestures, images, body language, and silence of the directee—in other words, by realities both spoken and unspoken—I note qualities and characteristics in my personal interior movements that flow from the Spirit of the Lord. What are the deeper implications of these reflections? What do I mean by them?

As a spiritual director, I have had a variety of personal experiences in my encounters with directees that have left an indelible impression on me. They are surely not infallible, but they are of such a nature that I cannot deny their reality nor raise any serious question about their meaning. From all of them I have come to know something of the presence, love, care, and wisdom of God. Together they have created within me an experience of the living God that is personal, unique, specific, and challenging. They have created within me too a complex reality consisting of image, feeling, concept, and intuition, a reality that I call my "God experience." I have learned critically to trust this experience as a sign or indicator of God's presence, action, and love of me. The experience carries a note of certainty, a self-justifying quality that I find trustworthy. Though at any given time I recognize the possibility of personal deception, generally the reminiscence or re-creation of this complex experience reveals the current action of God in myself or another.

Perhaps an example from another discipline will help clarify my meaning. Recently, there has been much work and experimentation in the field of parapsychology. In one experiment researchers attempted to sensitize a subject to the uniqueness and specificity of another human being. The working hypothesis is that the specific presence of any human being has a unique effect and impact on another human being, an effect that no other person can cause or duplicate. The subject is trained to examine the unique effect that one person has on another. Again, this is a very complex experience comprised of particular images, feelings, sensory reactions, concepts and intuitions, sights, scents, sounds, and experiences of "body energies," that is, the aura that each person projects. Gradually the subject becomes sensitive to the specificity of the other person. Once this is achieved, the subject, blindfolded and wearing earplugs, is brought into a room where a number of people are present. The researcher asks the subject two questions: Is there someone here that you know? Can you identify that person by standing in front of him or her? The subject is led through the room, but remember has had no sensory contact with anyone. Usually, the subject manages to locate and identify the person to whom he or she has been sensitized, if indeed the person is actually present in the room.

My "God experience" is in some fashion analogous to this particular experiment. God has a unique impact on me. By long and careful reflection, I have been able to describe how this God experience differs from the experience of another person, or from an aesthetic experience of art or music or natural beauty, or from any other heightened experience. Though I know and trust that others have had similar experiences of God, I realize from reflection, prayer, and conversation with my own spiritual director that my experience is specific, particular, and absolutely unique. I am convinced that nothing and no one apart from the presence and action of God can affect this particular experience in my consciousness. I cannot prove it to anyone, but I trust it as a part of my skills in spiritual direction and spiritual discernment.

I try to attend to this God experience in the spiritual direction encounter. When I say that the director must listen to individual experience almost as intently and intensely as listening to the faith-experience of the directee, I am, in fact, referring to the God experience. When the lived reality of the directee is touched by and informed by the Spirit of God, it touches harmoniously the God experience of the director as well, creating a renewal of the God experience within the director. This does not always happen; when it does occur, though, it usually involves varying levels of awareness and intensity. Whenever and however it occurs, it is immensely important for the director to attend to it, because it can point to a clear and accurate picture of a directee's experience. In short, the director's attention to a personal God experience can help the directee distinguish between the various strands of interior experience and to respond to those experiences that are initiated by the Spirit of God.

A practical application of these reflections implies that a director must become adept at personal discernment and must be a man or woman of good spirit. The director must become increasingly alert to and aware of individual interior movements and experiences. By prayer, personal reflection, and conversation with one's own spiritual director, a person conducting the ministry of direction must gradually hone and refine an inner sense of awareness of God's unique action in his or her life, so that this awareness can be made available to others as a touchstone for spiritual discernment.

These, then, are the realities of the careful and arduous processes of spiritual discernment that a director must recognize, specifically, the quality of the directee's spirit and the unique effect that the directee's self-revelation and self-communication has on the spirit of the director. Only by paying careful attention to these realities can the director assist the directee to assimilate, understand, and interpret the varied and sometimes subtle interior movements prompted by the Spirit of God. The director's God experience may be the most powerful resource available for a director in spiritual direction and spiritual discernment.

Strategies for Spiritual Discernment

I now turn briefly to some of the techniques used in spiritual discernment. These aids, hallowed by the Christian tradition, have been recommended with significant fruitfulness by countless generations of Christians. Perhaps their most classic usage appears as the Rules for Discernment in the *Spiritual Exercises* of Saint Ignatius. An immense amount of literature has been written on these rules. Opinion about their meaning and interpretation varies widely. It would be tedious in a practical work such as this to present a technical discussion. I will, however, offer some brief remarks about them in the hope they may aid both director and directee in the delicate work of spiritual discernment.

It is important to recognize the larger context in which the Rules for Discernment are placed. Ignatius believed that decision making is crucial to the life and growth of Christians. It is through decision making, he maintained, that we co-create with God our very selves. He therefore proposed ways in which we ordinarily make decisions under the guidance of the Spirit of God. In this context of Christian decision making, he formulated and utilized his Rules for Discernment. According to Ignatius, we can make the decisions that shape our life before the living God in three ways. Though he implied that these ways are independent and exclusive of one another, experience proves that they often overlap or complement. He describes these ways succinctly in the *Spiritual Exercises* and then offers practical aids to help in the decision-making process.

First, Ignatius speaks about an intuitive certitude that one has about an object of choice, an attraction that carries with it a convincing quality of truth. Though one may be unable to prove it, one has an inner confidence that is initiated, blessed, or inspired by God. Ignatius is describing here that privileged time of awareness or insight that many have experienced and which they have followed with courage, conviction, and commitment.

Many commentators on the *Spiritual Exercises* consider this first way of decision making to be relatively rare. It is exactly because it seldom occurs that it deserves careful scrutiny. I believe, though, that this way happens much more frequently than the literature suggests. Indeed, I find it to be a fairly common, though not ordinary, way of decision making. People do know, at least inchoatively, what they want and what is really in their best interest before God.

Second, Ignatius describes the way of consolation and desolation as a decision-making procedure, and it is here that he utilizes the Rules for Discernment. A decision-making procedure presumes that quite frequently we experience a time of alternating certainties and doubts, of exhilarating strength and debilitating weaknesses, of consolation and desolation. It also presupposes that these alternating inner realities form a gateway toward understanding a language of God spoken within our very being. I suggested this procedure earlier when I noted that similar spirits provoke harmony, peace, tranquility, and integration in the good-spirited person. These realities manifest a kind of inborn instinct between the Spirit of God and the directee, so that decisions that are Godward stimulate inner peace, harmony, and interior consolation.

Under this rubric the rules for spiritual discernment in the *Spiritual Exercises* are very useful. They provide practical guidelines and insights into the nature, value, and purposes of spiritual consolation. They are based on the premise that only God can initiate certain interior and subjective experiences. These experiences are called *consolations*. Though the experiences are not infallible, they do carry with them a dimension of certainty that one can readily and unequivocally identify with the action of God. They are ordinarily attributed to the presence and action of the Holy Spirit within the person. Decisions in harmony with or congruent to these inner experiences stimulate or provoke consolation. Decisions that turn one away from God lead to interior desolation. Father David L. Fleming, author of a book on the *Spiritual Exercises*, remarked, "When we are trying to follow the call of the Lord in our life, we will find that the good spirit tends to give support, engagement, and oftentimes even a certain delight in all our endeavors."

Experientially, I have found discernment by consolation and desolation to be the most ordinary and typical manner of discernment. People carry their personalized experience of God within them. They have access to an inner language that God initiates and that is "spoken" as spiritual consolation. It is a language that requires interpretation, but it is trustworthy and can lead to a pattern of choices and behaviors that bring one to the truest self and to the God that desires that truest self.

Ignatius's guidelines for discernment by consolation and desolation are subtle. They point to the possibility that we can misread, misinterpret, or misunderstand the origin, direction, or pattern of experiences. Despite their subtlety, though, they remain practical guidelines for this very common style of decision making. They help us to interpret with clarity and conviction the meaningful patterns of our interior movements.

A third method of decision making is that of prayerfully enlightened intelligence, often caricatured as the way of pros and cons. The decision maker collects and evaluates the advantages and disadvantages and from this evaluation chooses the alternative that seems most reasonable. The pro-and-con method is urged during a tranquil period when one is not moved in any palpable way by the Spirit of God. At such a time one weighs the matter carefully and prayerfully, attempting to choose a pattern of behavior that is reasonably consonant with the presence of God in one's life.

Although all these ways of discernment are treated as separate and different, they often overlap. I always find it helpful to use the third way, the way of prayerfully enlightened intelligence, even when clarity and conviction are present. Invariably, both the intuitive clarity of the first way and the consolation of the second weaken and fade. When they do, it is empowering to know the reasons and motives that abide and continue to support or even strengthen the decision(s) one has made. It has become rather common in our day to denigrate the role of reason and understanding in Christian decision making in favor of emotion and affect. I think this is a tragic mistake. Not that reason offers any greater clarity or insight than affect, but reason and affect working together can provide a powerful impetus to implement the life-giving decision to which they have given birth. Thus, as a director, I would always urge the way of enlightened reason and prudence, no matter how the decision was initially made.

Conclusion

The tradition and literature of prayer and discernment are extensive and incredibly rich. I have offered some personal and practical reflections on both as an aid to directors in their central tasks of prayer guidance and spiritual discernment. Their value lies in their practicality rather than their theoretical description.

Two more issues need to be addressed: the qualifications of the director and reflections on the actual process of spiritual direction. Thus, I will attempt to answer the following questions in the next chapter: who should do spiritual direction? and how does direction really work? Let us now turn our attention to these important topics.

Further Reading

David L. Fleming, S.J., *The Spiritual Exercises of St. Ignatius: A Literal Translation and a Contemporary Reading* (St. Louis, Mo.: Institute of Jesuit Sources, 1978).

John Futrell, S.J., "Ignatian Discernment," *Studies in the Spirituality of Jesuits* 2, no. 2 (February 1970).

Thomas H. Green, S.J., *Weeds Among the Wheat* (Notre Dame, Ind.: Ave Maria Press, 1984).

David J. Hassel, S.J., *Radical Prayer* (Mahwah, N.J.: Paulist Press, 1983).

Ernest Larkin, O. Carm., *Silent Presence* (Denville, N.J.: Dimension Books, 1981).

Jules Toner, S.J., *A Commentary on St. Ignatius' Rules for the Discernment of Spirits* (St. Louis, Mo.: Institute of Jesuit Sources, 1982).

_____, *Discerning God's Will* (St. Louis, Mo.: Institute of Jesuit Sources, 1991).

Ann and Barry Ulanov, *Primary Speech* (Atlanta: John Knox Press, 1982).

4

The Director and the Process of Direction

Throughout this work I have presumed that spiritual direction is a ministry that takes place within the Christian community. It is a service provided for the well-being of the community and its members. This means, of course, that it is a spiritual gift, a true charism, granted by God's Spirit for the growth and development of the Kingdom of God. Certainly learned skills, techniques, and abilities can facilitate this gift, but they can never replace it. The God-given gift of spiritual direction takes precedence over all other skills that a person has learned.

How, then, does one recognize this gift of the Spirit in oneself, and how does one know it as true charism? How does one assess personal gifts of direction and discernment before offering them to other Christians?

Community Recognition

Strange as the answer may seem, one does not recognize the gift of spiritual direction in oneself. It is initially and essentially recognized by those for whom it is needed and to whom it is directed by God. This gift of direction and spiritual discernment is noted and affirmed by those who seek one out to serve and minister to them as director and/or discerner. In other words, the community validates the gifts of spiritual directors and is the final arbiter of their authenticity and validity.

Too often we associate or identify the gift of direction with a particular role or office, such as a priest, a superior, a person with an advanced degree, and/or an elected official. The gift may reside in such persons, but not *because* of their role or office, their position or education. The gift or charism is different and distinct from any particular role or office, any specific work or ministry. The Spirit of God generously and abundantly scatters this gift to the people of God and makes it available where and as it is needed. Often we find it in the most surprised and surprising persons!

Therefore, the gift is affirmed by those for whom it is meant. How then does one know whether or not one has this gift for spiritual direction and spiritual discernment? Knowledge comes with a degree of clarity, and even some certitude, when members of the Christian community seek one another out to accompany them in their quest for the living God. It is the very prompting of the Spirit of God that leads a person to seek a particular and specific director for him- or herself.

The work of the Spirit has a great deal to do with the faith and trust that already exist in the Christian community, for very often a directee seeks out a particular director because of the experience, recommendation, or referral of someone whom he or she knows and trusts—a friend, confidant, former director, or trusted colleague. Eventually, it comes down to the simple fact that someone once trusted his or her interior movements and, on the basis and strength of these inspirations of grace, sought direction from a particular person and, gratefully, it worked.

The directee recognizes a gift of the Spirit in the prospective director that makes him or her credible and attractive. Some gifts speak to the person in a way that prompts the initial trust, confidence, and commitment necessary to begin fruitful spiritual direction and discernment. Once this occurs the person can recommend the director to others on the basis of lived personal experience. Reality of faith and trust within the community validates the gift of direction in particular persons within that community of lived faith.

Thus, awareness of the gift of direction arises at the juncture between divine call and human response, between grace and personal freedom. It is heard in the human needs that surround us. The gifts of direction and discernment are found in the needs of one's brothers and sisters in the Christian community, in one's natural aptitudes, and, ultimately, in the personal inclination to conduct a ministry. The fact that people seek out someone to do ministry can be a very powerful indication of the coming together of God's gifts and a personal response to those gifts.

At the same time, though, one ought to have a healthy feeling of inadequacy for the task without feeling paralyzed, since it means collaborating with the Spirit of God to touch the human heart—a truly delicate and awesome invitation.

That others sought direction is a good indicator that one *does* have the qualities and gifts people desire in a director, even if one has not done ministry before or thinks that now may not be the appropriate time to begin because of personal inadequacy. In fact, this could be *kairos*, a moment of grace for prospective directors and for the directees who seek their aid in the search for God.

Gifts Needed for Direction

What combination of gifts do members of the family of God seek in those to whom they go for spiritual direction and help in personal discernment? What makes a person competent in this ministry of direction and able to draw others with trust and confidence? Generally, these gifts are theological and psychological awareness, spiritual experience, and interpersonal skills. The following reflections should help.

Theological and Psychological Awareness

What do people look for and expect from those to whom they go for direction and spiritual discernment? There needs to be a balance in the areas of Scripture, the Christian ascetical and spiritual tradition(s), and recent advances in the human sciences, particularly psychology. The working presumption here is that God communicates through the revealed Word, through human experience, and through the various manifestations of human culture. Significant interplay exists between the various realities. A qualified director should have the basic knowledge to work with confidence in these three areas of the God-person relationship.

What level of competence is acceptable or most needful? One does not have to be a professionally trained Scripture scholar. Yet one should not be so unskilled in the meaning and pattern of Scripture that one is wholly unable to use the revealed Word as an object of prayer or an instrument in spiritual direction and discernment. From a practical perspective, this means knowing something about the various literary forms of the Bible, the thematic content of the revealed Word, current exegetical and hermeneutical advances, and techniques for interpreting the Word in our contemporary postmodern social context.

Qualified directors also need some theoretical and practical awareness of the Christian ascetical and spiritual tradition, which is almost as important as knowledge and awareness of the Bible itself. Knowledge and awareness protects the director from a narrow understanding or interpretation of the directee's experience. Awareness of the collective wisdom and insight of the Christian community prevents the director from imposing personal spiritual experiences as indicative of the rest of humankind. In addition, the richness of the tradition allows the director to adopt a variety of approaches that are uniquely and specifically adapted to the needs of a particular directee.

A director also needs knowledge of systematic spiritual theology and an awareness of the typical structures and functions in spiritual life. The Christian tradition includes a variety of spiritual experiences within the community of faith. It reveals the creative and diverse ways in which God communicates with people. It illuminates typical patterns of experience while supporting, encouraging, and blessing uniqueness and individuality.

People who seek a spiritual guide or companion expect psychological insight or at least a lived awareness of human dynamics. The need for fundamental knowledge of human psychology is based on Christian incarnation, which assumes that God works in and through the ordinary processes of human growth and development. In other words, it means that if people have personality traits that prevent them from loving others, they need psychological help. An apt spiritual director should be aware of at least some of these human obstacles and know how to deal with them. Again, what does this mean practically, since it would be unrealistic to expect that every spiritual director be a professionally trained psychologist or clinician? It simply means that the director should be familiar with one or another acceptable psychological theories of human personality and human development and be aware of the ordinary signs of human responsibility and human maturation—both masculine and feminine. Most important, the director should be able to recognize some of the typical symptoms of psychological or emotional disorder, disability, or disease. There should be some minimal recognition of the distinctly different developmental processes and psychological dynamics between men and women. Finally, it is of the utmost importance in order to protect the well-being of the directee, the credibility of spiritual direction, and the integrity of the clinical sciences for the director to have the humility and knowledge to recommend that emotionally troubled directees seek professional clinical intervention rather than using pop psychology to handle their problems.

In the particular area of psychological and human sciences awareness, I have discovered three different types of spiritual directors. The first type is only interested in the spiritual side of the directee. That is, the direction conversation only addresses the directee's prayer and practice of Christian virtue. For whatever reason, such a director is unable or unwilling to discuss any other dimensions of the directee's life and experience. A blatant kind of Platonism is apparent here. Work, ministry, community, family, personal relationships, leisure, emotional life, sexuality—all are explicitly and systematically filtered out of the encounter between director and directee, which essentially reduces spiritual direction to pious conversation. Often the director behaves this way because he or she has not prayerfully confronted these areas in his or her own life and is either afraid of or incapable of hearing them in the life and experience of others. I would categorically urge that such directors remove themselves from the ministry of spiritual direction. Their benign silence about the most important realities in human experience often creates more difficulties than they resolve.

The second type of director tends to err in the opposite direction. Essentially such directors equate spiritual direction with psychological counseling or psychotherapy. The therapeutic model applies here. The underlying presumption is that all will be right between directee and God when all is right intrapsychically or psychodynamically. These directors can be far more dangerous than the first type. They are often ill-prepared to pursue and resolve the emotional and/or psychological issues that they raise in their so-called spiritual direction. Generally, they are devotees of popular psychological journals and workshops but have little actual clinical experience and less awareness of their clinical limitations. Though this sounds very harsh, I am convinced that they give a bad name to both spiritual direction and psychotherapy, because they neither direct nor offer therapy. These directors, too, should disqualify themselves from the ministry of spiritual direction until they have studied the long and tedious work of learning the Christian spiritual and ascetical tradition and achieved an adequate competence level in psychology.

Finally, the third type is the only one that truly deserves the name of spiritual director. Because of the levels of awareness, knowledge, and competence that these directors possess, they represent the authentic Christian tradition of spiritual direction and discernment. They have familiarized themselves with the revealed Word of God to the degree that they can use it fruitfully in direction and discernment. They are in touch with the history, dynamics, and spirituality of the Christian tradition within the greater Christian community. They are knowledgeable about human relations, normal psychological development, and maturation and use this awareness as part of their ministry without reducing the work of direction and discernment to an offshoot of the clinical sciences. In short, they are at home in their own house and can therefore invite others—their directees—to a place where direction and discernment are truly possible.

Spiritual Experience

If knowledge of Scripture, the Christian tradition, and psychology constitute the first facet of a director's charism for discernment, then spiritual or faith experience form the second. Since this is a very practical ministry, the director ordinarily needs both personal experience of the Spirit and personal supervision in the ministry as well as personal spiritual direction for him- or herself. Indeed, recent literature about direction strongly emphasizes the need for both personal spiritual direction and supervision for anyone engaged in the ministry of direction. This experience is probably the most difficult dimension of readying oneself for the ministry, especially if one's past or earlier experience of spiritual direction has been negative. Whatever one's past, though, the felt need for personal direction and supervision may serve as the measuring rod of one's seriousness and purpose. Without personal direction and supervision, it is likely that an unreflected countertransference in the director will exert a powerful influence—positive or negative—on the directee. The influence can be so strong as to block the inner movements of the directee and interfere with the ordinary processes of spiritual direction. The director consistently needs to be aware of what is happening within him- or herself. The director needs also to own, assimilate, and integrate consciously his or her inner world and the actual work of spiritual direction. Both personal spiritual direction and ministerial supervision can help.

Supervision is not meant simply to be an academic or intellectual exercise that has no relationship to actual ministry. Rather it involves doing casework about the direction that one is doing. It leads to the examination of attitudes, projections, anxieties, and fears that one experiences in the spiritual direction relationship. It is the mechanism or technique that calls one to personal authenticity and honesty. Certainly for men and women just beginning the ministry of direction, such supervision is of the utmost importance. But it is also crucial for those with broad experience. I cannot stress enough the importance of personal direction and supervision for anyone engaged in this work. Generally, people are not qualified to *do* direction if they have not *had* direction because they do not or cannot respond to their own spiritual experience in an adequate fashion.

The religious experience of the director is of such vital concern in spiritual direction that it needs to be discussed in greater detail. What would I ordinarily include in a consideration of this experience?

Certainly the environment of faith that exists in the direction situation is important. Whatever the director says, feels, or does in the direction context takes place in an environment of faith. It is apparent in the air that he or she breathes, the music he or she hears, the garment he or she wears. The director should live the Christian life enthusiastically and vitally. The director should have a felt knowledge of salvation, of being loved by God, of loving others and being loved by them. The director should know experientially that salvation has been made available to him or her. The director should also realize that God is an authentic part of the direction process, that he or she is drawn into a deeper life with God in the ministry of direction.

The faith life and experience of the director also means that he or she belongs to a community of faith with others who together teach one another how to forgive and how to love, as God does. Community with others of similar values, cares, and commitments becomes a challenge for the director. The vision of others who are making Kingdom-directed decisions provides the director with the balance and challenge to do the same. The appetite of others for God whets a similar appetite within the director. The faith of the director is strengthened and nurtured by the faith that he or she shares with others in the larger community of faith.

Some directors yield rather easily to a kind of formalism in their ministry: they reduce the work to a set of learned skills and developed techniques that gradually degenerates into "canned" reactions to the directee. The only remedy is to embrace the environment of faith in the life of the director and in the actual ministry of direction. Only then will the director be saved from predetermined responses. In an environment of faith the director *knows* that he or she is in a collaborative process with both God and the directee to discover the most authentic and appropriate decisions for the directee.

Certainly the director must be a person of faithful and persistent prayer. The director prays from a sense of personal need for the gifts of sensitivity, insight, wisdom, availability to the Spirit, and balance and equilibrium. The director also prays to prevent interior stagnation. The great Spanish guitarist, Andrés Segovia, even into his eighties, practiced scales every day, to keep abreast of the most rudimentary musical skills. Prayer serves the same function for the director. The director needs prayer in order to be saved from personal blind spots and to remember that he or she is not God and savior, but rather an intermediate instrument of God.

The directee also needs the prayer of the director. Such prayer, if it is to be authentic, demands a commitment by the director to the well-being of the directee. Committed prayer enriches the directee in unimaginable ways.

In addition, the director needs to be consistently aware of his or her own sinfulness, prejudices, blind spots, addictions,

compulsions, and any other impediments to personal freedom. Some directors, for example, have a compulsive desire
to be needed that turns them into intrusive problem solvers
or dispensers of vapid advice. If the director is not mindful of
such needs, he or she could easily move into very inappropriate behavior, such as manipulating the decision making of
the directee or trying to fix the directee's problems. The director becomes overly parental, creating attachments and
unfreedoms that do not empower the freedom and growth of
the directee. In some directors this could become a serious
professional disorder. The director needs to be able to distinguish individual needs from the needs of the directee. The
director has a professional obligation not to allow personal
needs to manipulate or control the direction session. Directors must always remember that the directee is not there to
take care of their needs.

The director must be sensitive to personal needs yet be
careful not to abuse the direction relationship in order to
meet them. Fatigue, for example, often leads to agitation,
anxiety, and lack of focus or sensitivity, which can, in turn,
disrupt the direction process. Better for the director to rest
and become physically and psychologically ready to offer a
focused presence than burden the directee with one's own
unmet needs.

In their own spiritual experience directors must also allow
God to confront their false expectations, their prejudices and
biases, their stereotypes involving various kinds of directees.
We all have our own interior mechanisms—irrational though
they may be—that negatively characterize people because of
race, sex, age, or station in life. Such stereotypical expectations color, determine, and negatively control the process of
spiritual direction. In actual practice authentic experience
reveals the invalidity of these stereotypes. Still, the director
must labor to eradicate all false expectations and negative
categories from him- or herself.

At the same time, the director must recognize deeply felt
values and convictions. It becomes very easy to communi-

cate these values, which are very dear to one's heart, inappropriately to the directee. The director does not have the right to impose them on the directee. In short, the director has to be highly sensitive to the history, temperament, personality, and grace of each directee and God's specific call while communicating new areas and issues of Christian responsibility.

The faith life and experience of the director must also lead to increased interior freedom. Some directors covet immediate results. But they are headed for trouble and often provoke a good deal of frustration in their directees. They usually rush in where they do not belong and spoil the unique timing, the kairos, of God's Spirit. It does require a unique kind of interior freedom to trust God's timing.

Interior freedom also includes freedom from fear of the directee. This fear or awe can and often does prevent much good from taking place and can be a severe temptation to directors who are diffident about their gifts for the ministry. That is, it limits their potential as directors and narrows their ability to hear God's call to the directees whom they hold in such awe. They must learn to maintain their role and offer their experience and expertise, limited though it is, in simple faith and trust. If they remain unwilling to acknowledge their own gifts and talents, they will severely limit their effectiveness as an instrument of God in the ministry of direction.

Finally, the director needs to be able to address both sides of a question, to tolerate ambiguity. The director must have the ability to sift the good and the valuable from the dross, to get inside the skin of the directee and hear and see things from his or her perspective. This ability can lead to the realization that sometimes things are not always what they seem and that waiting patiently may be the only recommendation that can be offered to the directee. The director with an exaggerated need for clarity or closure may find such behavior difficult, but it is really the only way to be truly helpful.

Giving competent direction is a matter of being cooperative with grace—not getting in the way of God's action—

being sensitive to persons in their uniqueness and their circumstances. It involves an inner discipline that allows God to work with the directee, sufficient intelligence and self-knowledge to know what one does not know, and a willingness to study, learn, and grow into an ever deeper ability to listen to the Spirit of God.

For all of this to be accomplished, every director needs a life of prayer, a context of shared faith in community, time for study and holy leisure, and a deeply reflective attitude toward life. There is need for constant learning and a willingness to listen to the rhythms of life, the movements of one's heart, and the whispers of God's Spirit.

Interpersonal Skills

The gift or charism for direction and discernment is indicated by the quality of a director's interpersonal skills. This may seem obvious, yet it is something that is often taken for granted or, worse, forgotten. Years ago Henri Nouwen suggested the rubric of hospitality to describe the type of relationship necessary for successful ministry to occur. I, too, see hospitality as a key factor that must exist between director and directee if a ministry is to develop in a fruitful and meaningful manner.

What shape or contours does the hospitality of spiritual direction take in this very privileged relationship? Hospitality is a virtue that allows us to break through the narrowness of our own fears, our own biases and prejudices, our own parochial concerns. Hospitality invites us to open our inner and outer "houses" to the stranger with the realization that salvation also comes to us in the form of the weary and tired fellow-pilgrim. Hospitality is the human ability to focus on and pay attention to someone else, such as the directee. This can be very difficult, since often we are preoccupied with our own needs, which can prevent us from maintaining the proper distance from ourselves in order to pay attention to others. When directors are restless in spirit, when they are driven by countless conflicting stimuli, when they live outside of their own centers, how can they possibly create the safe room and hospitable space where a directee can enter freely without feeling like an unlawful intruder?

It is terribly important, therefore, that directors periodically withdraw inward to create the safe space for directees to be themselves and enable them to come to direction in honest and simple trust. Only when directors find an anchor for their own lives can they be free to let others enter into their sacred space and allow them to dance their own dance, sing their own song, speak their own language, and find their own God without fear.

The director who has this gift of hospitality and is at ease with him- or herself can offer a safe haven. Often all a directee really seeks is security and safety. The director offers a friendly space, where directees can feel free to come and go, to be close or distant, to rest or play, to talk or be silent, to eat or fast, and, ultimately, to find inner peace. The wonderful paradox is that the directee can find his or her own soul and spirit in the empty space of the director's hospitality.

When directees enter such space, they see that they can also enter their own hearts and spirits without personal fear. They begin to understand that illusions, false self-expectations, personal masks, and roles can be put aside safely, so that their real personhood can emerge honestly and beautifully. They find support and encouragement rather than judgment or moral critique. They discover the possibility of deliverance from age-old fears and compulsions in an atmosphere of affirmation that is free from judgment or preaching. All of this is available to them only if and when they find a safe and hospitable place to put down their burdens and honestly and securely reveal themselves.

Self-Appropriation

Another way to understand the development of interpersonal trust that makes spiritual direction possible is to examine self-appropriation. To do the ministry of spiritual direction, one must "own oneself." "Owning" oneself is a dimension of personal experience, not simply intellectual knowledge or unctuous affirmation of the director by others. The director experiences an awareness of deeply felt personal convictions that ground self-appropriation and self-ownership. This self-appropriation and self-ownership begins with competence. From experience one learns that there are some things one does as well or better than other people. It is not simply that others say a person does things well. Rather one has an interior barometer, a learned set of performance criteria that create a personal sense of competence. It is not necessary to hear affirmation from others to bolster self-esteem.

Further, one has an experienced awareness of personal goodness. Certainly, one's past liabilities, failures, mistakes, and sins can diminish the interior awareness of personal goodness—the awareness of a good mind, a good heart, holy desires, and personal gifts. Yet, one holds firmly and deeply to personal conviction and communicates to the world with confidence.

Self-appropriation has an interpersonal dimension in the realization that one has affected others for the good, which implies that some people are clearly better for knowing a particular person in their lives. It is not a question of action or behavior. Rather it is one's personal goodness, the quality of one's life and person, that has had a positive influence on the lives of other people. Thus, one has no need to seek positive feedback from others.

An inner sense of personal direction completes the portrait of the self-appropriated man or woman. The person experiences a positive conviction about the shape of one's own life while being, of course, attentive to the needs, expectations, requests, and demands of others. But these outside interests never take priority or precedence over inner direction. Self-appropriated individuals have an inner vision of who they are and who they are becoming. It is to this vision that one must be true. Thus, the person does not rely on authority, status, or achievement for personal validation.

Self-appropriated men and women elicit trust from others because of the quality of self that they project in all that they say and do. It is this kind of person who will most often be chosen by members of the Christian community to companion others in their journey of faith.

The Process of Spiritual Direction

We must turn now to the dynamics of spiritual direction. How does the spiritual direction relationship work? What propels or drives it? What makes for successful direction? Conversely, what inhibits such direction? I will again try to provide some practical and descriptive answers to these important questions.

Central to the dynamics of the relationship is the actual person of the director. Faith, hope, and love and the capacity to form a trusting and meaningful relationship become crucial for the success of spiritual direction. The director must realize that spiritual direction is the *work of God* being done by a *most important human instrument*. A fine line exists here: spiritual direction is not a director's work, but, on the other hand, the director's presence is crucial. A director's unique gifts and talents are important during the actual process of spiritual direction.

How, then, does a fruitful relationship occur? The directee needs to have a deep desire to grow in the life of the Spirit, a desire for the fullness of life that God also desires. This desire joins the gifts and talents of the director and creates a covenant between them—a committed agreement to collaborate for the desired growth of the directee. Both parties sense intuitively and respect the desire for fullness of life in the directee, and both commit to work together to attain that desire, whatever the cost. This covenanted relationship sustains the directee in the sometimes difficult work of seeking God; it empowers the director to commit and devote time, talent, energy, and patience to the same goal.

The directee's desire and longing for God is the basis for the mutual covenant in the spiritual direction relationship. This desire is powerful and energizing. It allows the directee persistently and steadfastly to confront deep-seated personality and character traits that prevent important collaborative work from being fruitful. The faith, hope, and love of the director respond to the directee's desire for a fuller life, forging a dynamic bond that can withstand the inevitable difficulties of the relationship and the inherent demands that exploring a true growth in the Lord require. This dynamic and empowering bond between director and directee is indeed the driving force of the entire process of spiritual direction.

The Christian tradition has consistently attributed desire for growth in the directee and hope in the director to the presence and action of God's Spirit. In the Christian profession of faith God is addressed as "the Lord, the Giver of life." It is the presence and action of God's Spirit that gives the deepest meaning to spiritual direction, that is, the direction of one's spirit by God's Spirit. The intrapsychic and interpersonal dynamics of the spiritual direction relationship, therefore, are grounded in the powerful and life-giving action of the Holy Spirit in conjunction with the gifts of the director and the desires of the directee.

Rogerian psychology offers some insight into the inner dynamics of the spiritual direction relationship and the process of spiritual direction. The working presumption is based on the belief that all human beings have within them a minimal capacity for constructive growth, self-direction, and maturation. A vital force in each person moves toward a fuller life and an actualization of the self. To use theological terminology, the gifts of the Spirit as seen in faith, hope, and charity are part of and supportive of the inner personal inclination to self-actualization, which is the vital thrust to becoming a fully integrated person. This self-actualization drive resides in the directee. It can be nurtured by an atmosphere of genuineness, caring, and understanding that is created by the director. Direction succeeds and is fruitful as a process when the director provides this atmosphere, so that the directee's potential for self-direction and self-actualization can be released. The director needs to find, support, and facilitate the gifts that are already present in the directee.

The director's genuineness, caring, and understanding help the directee to discover and respond to the guidance of God's Spirit who is urging one to seek a fuller life. The director is the instrument rather than the cause of growth. This truth protects the director from any inclination to self-aggrandizement or a tendency to adopt a "savior" complex. The director helps to remove obstacles that inhibit the self-actualization of the directee, creating the atmosphere that allows personal direction and actualization to occur.

The human tendency to want to develop one's personal gifts and talents to their fullest allows the directee to experience psychologically the Spirit's guidance to God and best sums up the meaning of Saint Irenaeus' famous statement that the glory of God is the human person fully alive.

What are the qualities in the director that facilitate self-actualization and growth in the directee? What exactly does genuineness, caring, and understanding mean?

The Director's Genuineness, Caring, and Understanding

Genuineness is a personal authenticity, being oneself as fully as one can in the relationship of direction. It entails a director's continual awareness of personal experience, which include feelings, images, reactions, and attitudes that emerge in the direction situation. It also involves the freedom to communicate this awareness to the directee, especially when these emotions persist over a protracted period of time. It means being honest with oneself and the directee. The directee knows that "what you see is what you get" in the direction relationship. There is no hidden agenda. The director, to whatever degree possible, is aware and conscious of him- or herself and honestly communicates the true self to the directee.

Honest caring in the spiritual direction relationship is possible but somewhat more difficult. To care means to have an unconditional, positive reverence and unqualified acceptance of a unique person with the strengths and weaknesses that characterize that uniqueness. Directors have to work at this. God alone cares and accepts all of us unconditionally. We humans can only approximate it. Unconditional love means that the director places no conditions or expectations on the directee that have to be met or fulfilled to merit or earn the director's affirmation, acceptance, or esteem. It implies respect and a nonpossessive love for the person as he or she is; it asks the director to exercise true charity. It also means, as Saint Paul recommends, that we speak the truth with love. It is not necessary that a director *like* every directee, though this can help a great deal. What it does mean is that directors need to pray for a deepened gift of real charity, love, and genuine care for their directees.

Finally, the understanding of the director is necessary to create the atmosphere that facilitates the self-actualization, inner growth, and development of the directee. Understanding enables the director to respect the interior experience of the directee as if it were his or her own. It requires the director to enter the inner world of the directee without losing personal objectivity. In an effort to understand, the director struggles to see life as the directee does from his or her vantage point. The director seeks to understand accurately and sensitively the experiences, images, and symbols that affect the directee and the particular meanings that the directee attaches to them.

For the spiritual direction relationship to be successful, the emotions of the director must be authentic. They cannot be feigned or bogus. They must reflect the real experiences of the director. For example, a director who feels agitated while conveying serenity or shows admiration when feeling the opposite is being insincere. Similarly, to believe to have empathetically entered the experience of a directee when one has only a conceptual awareness shows a lack of respect for the directee's interior life. It is highly unlikely that real growth will develop in the directee under these circumstances. If spiritual direction is to benefit the directee, the director must pray for and develop the gifts as they are given by God.

The directee must be able to perceive these qualities in the director. If not possible, then growth and freedom will not occur. The direction process bears fruit to the degree that the director marshals these qualities and brings them to the ministry of direction. Whatever model of direction is used, the degree of effectiveness of the relationship *always* depends on the degree of authenticity, caring, and awareness one brings to the relationship. The various activities of direction—praying and teaching, advising and instructing, discerning and evaluating—facilitate the directee's spiritual growth only to the extent that an honest relationship exists. On the way to Emmaus, Jesus understood the experience of the disciples. He demonstrated genuineness and authenticity, which made it possible for them to grow in freedom and discipleship.

Criteria for Evaluating Spiritual Direction

The director must have objective criteria to evaluate the effectiveness of the direction that is being offered. What ought one look for when making such an evaluation? What indicates a fruitful spiritual direction relationship?

Certainly altruism is a sign of growth in the directee. Altruism entails a new or deepened awareness of others, a sensitivity to and absorption in the reality of other human beings. It marks a shift from egocentrism to awareness of and positive regard for others. Altruism is the lived expression of charity and, as such, indicates the directee's growth and development in the Lord.

A deepening sense of hope in the directee is also a sign of growth. The directee discovers meaning and value in the present that offers support for a brighter future. As real collaboration with the authentic desires of the directee occurs, the directee's life takes on color and vibrancy. Rote and repetition give way to more creative options for the future. Hope flourishes.

Another sign of growth is a directee's ability to express feelings in an appropriate and authentic manner. Feelings long dormant or suppressed become available as a new source of creative energy. There is less embarrassment about emotional expression and more confidence in allowing true feelings to emerge. Emotional awareness can often have a cathartic effect, so that healing of past emotional hurts are experienced. There is greater "bounce" in life because of the rich emotions that are now available.

Trust in God and surrender to the working of the Spirit of God becomes more conscious for the directee. The awareness of mystery supports trust and empowers a free and intentional surrender. The result is less living by chance and more responsibility for decisions and their consequences. Because trust is placed in the guiding action of the Holy Spirit, decision making becomes more assured.

Issues of Transference in Spiritual Direction

Many things can disrupt the quality of the spiritual direction relationship—fatigue, impatience, biases or prejudices of the director and/or the directee, a lack of clarity about the nature of the relationship. Most of these issues can be negotiated without actually impeding its quality. One relational dynamic in particular, however, can wreak havoc and needs to be examined at length—transference.

In transference the directee sees the director in dual roles—as a loving or punishing parent, a harsh or approving taskmaster, an affirming or rejecting lover, a competitive or abusive sibling, a bossy or accepting authority figure. The directee attaches or transfers distorted images, feelings, memories, and experiences to the director. The directee feels strong, intense, and often very inappropriate feelings toward the director that have little or nothing to do with him or her. In this way, anger, rage, fear, anxiety, sadness, joy, love, hatred, and sexual feelings may be transferred to the director. The director does not warrant and does not elicit such an intense response. The director simply becomes the object or catalyst for feelings that are transferred to him or her from another person or situation.

Transference is of the utmost importance in therapeutic clinical work. Ordinarily transference is a significant part of the healing process in psychological therapy or clinical counseling. Eliciting transferential material and reactions is part of the professional competence and gift of a skilled therapist. The ability to identify and sustain transference is often crucial to emotional healing. Therefore, it is often incumbent on the therapist to allow, encourage, and actively promote transferential reactions in the client. More often than not, the direction and progress of therapy depends on the quality and intensity of transference. Thus, the competence level of the therapist and the quality of the relationship between client and therapist will often determine the level of progress.

This situation does not apply in spiritual direction, however. Emotional transference disrupts the direction process. It blurs the focus by devoting and even fixating too much of the directee's attention and emotional and spiritual energy on the director rather than on the directee's relationship with God. Remember, the point of spiritual direction is not the directee's relationship with the director but his or her relationship with the living God. Therefore, there is good reason to suspect transference when the directee spends a disproportionate amount of time focusing in prayer or in actual direction on the director or on the quality of their relationship. Transference invariably spells trouble for the spiritual direction relationship.

A number of factors contribute significantly to the development of transference in the therapeutic relationship. Generally speaking, the therapist does not engage in any serious self-revelation to the client. The client knows or understands very little about the life, temperament, or history of the therapist, except perhaps his or her professional training, clinical qualifications, and therapeutic competence. Because the therapist is so "opaque," he or she becomes a blank screen for the client. There is nothing by which to characterize the person of the therapist but his or her professional role. Thus, the client can project or transfer to this blank screen the images, feelings, and memories of the past and find a safe way to identify, examine, and resolve his or her emotional history. For these reasons it is very important that the therapist maintain a veil of anonymity with the client in order to develop the critical processes of psychological transference.

Further, the frequency of interactions between the client and the therapist often facilitates clinical transference. Generally, the more frequently the client consults the therapist, the more probable it is that an intense and highly therapeutic clinical transference will occur. Conversely, clinical transference is less likely when there is diminished frequency of contact between client and therapist. This situation explains the almost daily encounters that form the substance of classical Freudian analysis.

Neither of these factors is at play in spiritual direction. Ordinarily, spiritual direction has a conversational quality about it in which each person is involved and to which each makes a personal contribution. Self-revelation by the director is permissible and often very helpful to the directee. The personal faith experience of the director can illuminate or confirm a similar faith experience of the directee. Thus, the director can place his or her insights or difficulties, successes or failures, gifts or weaknesses at the service of the directee. In no sense, then, does the director serve as an anonymous blank screen. The directee must enter into dialogue with a real flesh-and-blood human being with a real history and all the strengths and weaknesses of other humans. This kind of interpersonal dialogue is well calculated to avoid most of the pitfalls of psychological transference.

Moreover, the pattern of frequent meetings so typical of clinical encounters is ordinarily absent from the spiritual direction relationship. In the process of regular spiritual direction the director meets with the directee approximately every two or three weeks. In a time of serious decision making or personal crisis, the meetings may occur more frequently or during the course of a protracted retreat when the director is meeting with the retreatant on a daily basis. In a retreat setting the director must use more than ordinary caution to avoid any emotional transference from the directee. But the regular pattern of meetings is far less frequent that what occurs in therapy or psychological counseling. Less frequency helps forestall the possibility of emotional transference in the relationship.

Even with these precautions, however, transference does sometimes occur. The emotional energy and conscious focus of the directee shifts from the relationship to God to the relationship with the director or the actual person of the director. Prayer, reflection, and the time given to direction become more centered on and preoccupied with the director. Presuming, of course, that the director has done nothing consciously to promote emotional transference, what is he or she to do when such transference occurs? What can help in such a situation?

There is no easy solution to this difficult problem, but some things may be useful. First, it is important for the director to remain alert, attentive, and reflective both during and after the encounter. Only by attention and alertness during the direction conversation can the director notice the subtle shifts that indicate the beginning of transference. The sooner that the director notices the warning signs, the more easily and quickly can they be resolved.

Supervision is extremely important and helpful to the director in avoiding and/or dealing with the problem of transference. An open and candid relationship with a supervisor can readily help directors to notice events in direction that they could easily miss by too much reliance on their own reflection. A competent supervisor is one of the best resources for even a very experienced director, because the supervisor's function is to insure that the spiritual direction processes and relationship maintain the correct focus, that is, a focus on the directee's relationship with God, not the relationship with the director. Often it is the attentive supervisor who first notes the relational shift that marks the inception of transference and supports the director in the very delicate and sophisticated process of confronting it as honestly as possible.

Once the director suspects transference, the best approach is an immediate but gentle confrontation. Truth and honesty remain one of the greatest gifts that the director can offer the directee. A truthful attempt to help the directee to refocus attention and energy toward the relationship with God is of the utmost importance. Renewed and persistent attempts to seek the presence and action of God in prayer and other life events is often sufficient to refocus the directee's energies and emotional preoccupations. Sometimes praying together for the presence and gift of God's Spirit during direction is enough to call the directee back to the goals and purposes of the direction relationship.

Failing these more gentle attempts at confrontation, the director may have to resort to a stronger and more direct form of intervention. It may become necessary to directly identify the shift that has occurred in the directee. In doing so the director should cite good examples of the shift as well as describe the changes that have occurred in prayer. Other issues to bring to the forefront include the increasing direction time that the directee has spent discussing the director and the frequent expression of intense and inappropriate feelings that the directee is experiencing toward the director. In short, the director should be able to list specific data and cite concrete examples that demonstrate the affective and emotional shift that has occurred. Often, in order to present a coherent and cogent case, collecting such information will require careful tracking over a lengthy period of time.

Even a gentle statement by the director on transference will often provoke denial, resistance, rationalization, or embarrassment in the directee. The intensity of the denial may alarm the director, but it is often the best indicator that significant transference does indeed exist. The director must be especially prayerful, courageous, and steadfast. The director must clearly focus on the well-being of the directee and on reestablishing the covenanted alliance between the director, the directee, and the Spirit of God. A direct and persistent approach can do much to resolve the transference and focus the direction relationship in an ordered and appropriate fashion.

Sometimes, though, transference continues and even worsens. Nothing that the director does can break the directee's preoccupation. Nothing diffuses the transferential quality of the relationship. This situation is one of the most difficult and painful experiences for both director and directee, for it always means that the relationship must be terminated. The working alliance that drives spiritual direction has been irreparably damaged. No longer can one assume that the purposes of direction can be attained. No longer is it possible for the director to facilitate the relationship with God because he or she has become the emotional and affective focus of the directee's awareness.

Clearly, the director must manage termination with tact, sensitivity, and gentleness. Speaking the truth with love is of paramount importance. Once the transference is acknowledged and the director and directee have been unable to refocus their mutual energy on the directee's relationship with God, termination should be done as quickly as possible.

Neither temporizing nor procrastination are helpful; a clean and definitive break must be made. Certainly, the director can refer the directee to another competent director and perhaps even arrange the initial meeting with a new director. But his or her relationship with the directee must be terminated for the well-being of the directee. Delay only makes the termination more difficult.

Since transference is always a serious possibility in the spiritual direction relationship, it behooves the director to be alert even to any slightest indication of it. The largest part of the responsibility for monitoring and avoiding transference invariably lies with the director. Directors must maintain vigilance and a contemplative posture about every direction relationship. Similarly, directors must reflect regularly on every spiritual direction relationship and be honest about any indications of emotional or affective transference. They must also exercise the utmost care not to do or say anything that might encourage transference.

Directors must also be alert to the possibility of countertransference. In countertransference the director fixates emotionally on the directee. The director then loses sight of the directee's well-being, leaving behind the covenant and cooperative alliance with the directee and the Spirit of God. Intense and inappropriate feelings are transferred to the directee; the foundation of the spiritual direction relationship is undermined. Countertransference demands honesty and truth in the director. Invariably it leads to the termination of the relationship, too, since very few directors have the objectivity and emotional skill to disengage their feelings and emotions.

Frequent contact with a directee in a nonprofessional setting often leads to countertransference. Avoiding any form of socializing with the directee is one way to lessen the possibility of countertransference in the spiritual direction relationship.

Gender Differences in Spiritual Direction

One final point regarding the inner dynamics of the spiritual direction relationship deserves our consideration. Important gender differences exist, and these differences must always be taken into account by the director. The gender of both the director and directee will influence the dynamics and quality of the spiritual direction encounter. I want to avoid any stereotyping of either gender, but it seems clear to me that men and women approach spiritual direction quite differently. Male directors also direct differently than do female directors. Female directees communicate and react differently and have different emphases in spiritual direction than do male directees. A competent director must remain conscious of these differences in the spiritual direction relationship.

Too often strictly male models and styles of direction, prayer, and relational interaction were held up as the norm for personal growth in the Spirit. The genuinely feminine experience was either misunderstood or discounted. The ministry of spiritual direction was considered the sole prerogative of men with the subsequent trivialization of the considerable gifts, insights, and lived experiences of women. Fortunately, the situation is changing dramatically. Today many women conduct spiritual direction ministry with the utmost competence and in ways that are appropriate to the feminine perspective and ethos. Much of the best current literature about prayer, direction, and interpersonal relationships has been authored by women. New images and symbols of God derived from the distinctive experience of women are a significant part of the current conversation about direction. Significantly, less hierarchical or patriarchal models are used in spiritual direction.

I will not yield to the temptation to engage in either the male-bashing that marks some of the more extreme feminist critiques or the dismissal of the feminine experience that has been typical of the more traditional and masculine understanding of the spiritual direction relationship. Since much has already been written about spiritual direction from a purely masculine and patriarchal perspective, I want to highlight briefly a few of the new and fruitful aspects of the spiritual direction relationship that have developed from distinctly feminine reflections.

A new language about spiritual direction is emerging from the experience of women, which is no small achievement. Throughout this work I have used the traditional language of director and directee because the language is so readily accessible to both men and women. However, it contains elements of an unequal and nonmutual style of relationship. It implies a kind of master-disciple relationship. Though I have tried to temper these inequities by presenting the spiritual direction relationship in as unbiased a way as possible, traditional usage remains at the heart of the direction process. For this reason, women are inclined to use a different set of terms. More familiar and relational language has become increasingly common. Words and phrases such as "soul friend," "spiritual companion," "co-discerner," or "fellow pilgrim" are now part of the ordinary parlance of direction. It shows both a shift in the language about direction and a shift in the actual practice of direction.

The language shift indicates, too, a need for mutuality to exist in the relationship. It calls for the breakdown of hierarchical or patriarchal dimensions. It opens up the spiritual direction relationship to explore *mutual* revelation and share a great deal more than the traditional masculine models have allowed or accepted. The language also encourages reverence between director and directee.

The language indicates other shifts in emphases about the processes of the direction relationship. The traditional masculine model, for example, has tended to emphasize understanding, analysis, and intellectual knowledge. Though the male approach alluded to the emotional and affective dimensions of human experience, it was often accompanied by suspicion. Traditional male models tend to flow from a neo-Platonic dualism, which seek a kind of stoic apathy that essentially represses the emotional life of the directee. This way of understanding diminishes both the affective reality and the physical component of the human person. Neither one does much service to the directee's well-being.

The feminine contribution has been significant. By physiology and hormonal structure women tend to be more grounded in the physical. Body awareness and wholeness of body and spirit are the rule rather than the exception for most women. Although integration of the physical, the intellectual, the emotional, and the spiritual is the life quest for many men and women, women have a head start on their journey to integration because of their higher physical and emotional awareness.

Thus, women directors are much more attentive to physical and emotional issues not only in the processes of spiritual direction but also in the actual spiritual direction relationship. This is not to say, of course, that women directors are less rational, intelligent, or competent than men nor is it to imply that they discount the rational in the lived experience of the directee. It does suggest, however, that they are more integrated in their approach to spiritual direction—both as directors and as directees.

Since the goal of direction is discerned decision making— that is, directees consistently make decisions in conjunction with their personal, specific, and unique experience of God, self, and others—women directors and directees are often freer of the pragmatic style of decision making that frequently characterizes male directors and directees. Women are far more attentive to the impact of the physical and the emotional in the decision-making process. Certainly they are far more sensitive to the effect that their personal decisions will have on other human beings.

The importance that women invest in mutuality, affect, and physicality underlines another rich dimension of their unique contribution to the understanding of spiritual direction. Making connections and exploring relationships are of primary value. Intuitively, women understand that the Kingdom of God is about human relationships. They know that God's reign is not a cause or an institution, a set of issues or truths. God's reign is relational, and relational connections are of ultimate importance. The connections between human beings, the animal kingdom, the environment, and the entire cosmos are also of immense importance in feminine consciousness and thus have a significant place in spiritual direction done by or for women.

Because of these emerging strands of authentic feminine consciousness, women have increasingly played an important role in social justice, social concerns, and ecological issues. These life-embracing and life-nurturing issues will, of course, necessarily come to the fore in any spiritual direction by or for women. Therefore, it is of paramount importance that both male and female directors keep these issues and concerns in the forefront of consciousness in the direction of women.

Feminine experience is also involved with human liberation. Increasingly both women and men are deeply concerned about freedom from hierarchy and patriarchy so that a new and liberated awareness of God and other human beings can emerge. This liberation implies very strong inclinations to the spontaneous, the creative, the life-giving, and the life-nurturing. The long-term effects of liberated awareness are now only dimly imagined. They remain a powerful vision and hope for many women. Male and female spiritual directors must labor to keep their potential alive in directees, because this too is the work of the Spirit of God.

The feminine experience of God is often notably different from the spiritual experiences of most men. Some believe that the mothering and feminine face of God is central only to women's experience in prayer. Yet researchers Carol Gilligan and theologians Rosemary Radford Ruether and Elizabeth Johnson have exposed the fallacy of this misguided conception. It is time for *all* spiritual directors, both men and women, to welcome and nurture the distinctive feminine experience of God in prayer, worship, and life. Clearly no human conception of God will ever be adequate to comprehend the reality of the Divine. But we would all be strengthened, enriched, and energized by the distinctive experience of women in prayer.

Failure to attend to the distinctive gender differences will predictably have a negative effect on the inner dynamics of the spiritual direction relationship. Female or male directees who are aware of these feminine and feminist concerns will not be well served by any director who is not equally aware of them. Such inattention will not only inevitably disrupt the spiritual direction relationship but also make it difficult, if not impossible, for the director and directee to form the constructive and collaborative alliance that nurtures a fruitful relationship.

Supervision for Spiritual Directors

In conclusion I want again to highlight the importance of supervision for those engaged in the ministry of spiritual direction. After many years of experience, I am profoundly convinced of the need for supervision for all directors, whatever their age, experience, training, or competence level. Nothing is more important than establishing and maintaining a mature, healthy, and fruitful relationship of spiritual direction.

I recommend either individual or group supervision, both of which involve honesty, openness, and integrity on the part of the director and the supervisor. Techniques such as role-playing and case studies are of special value in ministerial supervision. Mutual sharing of new insights on prayer, spiritual discernment, Christian decision making, and human development are also worthwhile aspects.

It is helpful for directors to have competent psychological or psychiatric professionals available as a reference. These people serve the director in two related ways. First, they act as a kind of supervisor, informing the director of various psychological dynamics and issues that do not ordinarily form a part of the director's personal competence. Second, they are available to provide psychological or psychiatric help to directees who are in need of professional assistance. Often directees suffering from emotional distress or psychological disease are unable or unwilling to find assistance by themselves. They more readily trust the insight and competence of a spiritual director and will seek an interview with a professional therapist if the therapist is trusted and respected by the director.

Conclusion

Much is expected from a competent spiritual director. High expectations, however, should not frighten anyone from following an authentic call to do this important ministry. As in all things, God is the initiator and the author of all the gifts needed to accomplish the work of direction. Even as the directee is invited to enter a relationship with great trust, so the director is called by God to trust the invitation. Only then will God's people find the spiritual direction that they need and long for.

Further Reading

William A. Barry, S.J., and William Connolly, S.J., *The Practice of Spiritual Direction* (New York: Seabury Press, 1982), 121–74.

Kathleen Fischer, *Women at the Well* (Mahwah, N.J.: Paulist Press, 1988).

Carol Gilligan, *In a Different Voice* (Cambridge, Mass.: Harvard University Press, 1982).

Sally B. Purvis, "Christian Feminist Spirituality," in *World Spirituality*, vol. 18, ed. Louis Dupre and Don E. Saliers (New York: Crossroad, 1989), 500–19.

Carl Rogers, "Client-Centered Psychotherapy," in *Comprehensive Textbook of Psychiatry II,* 2nd ed., ed. Alfred M. Freeman, Harold Kaplan, and Benjamin J. Saddock (New York: Williams and Wilkins, 1975), 1831–43.

Conclusion

No treatment of spiritual direction will ever be the last word. The mysteries of God and the human person constantly defy rational description and analysis. God will always loom larger and more mysterious than our limited abilities can imagine. Daily we learn more about the secrets of the human person and the human heart. The more we learn about God and the human person, the more there is to learn.

Guided by the Spirit is a modest attempt to address the mystery of God and the human person and the relationship between the two. Its aim is to further the dialogue about spiritual direction. Though this work has offered some insight into the ministry of direction spiritual development, prayer, discernment, the process of direction—still much remains to be done. The complicated questions of human awareness and human motivation, the relationship between direction and psychological therapy, new insights into prayer and spiritual discernment, the impact of non-Christian religious thought and practice on spiritual direction—all of these and more need serious study and analysis to enhance the actual practice of pastoral ministry.

In many ways *Guided by the Spirit* is only a beginning, a small but significant contribution to understanding effective spiritual direction. Surely it raises as many questions as it answers about the direction process. Above all, it highlights repeatedly the importance and need of spiritual direction.

It is my deepest hope and prayer that *Guided by the Spirit* will be helpful and constructive for all spiritual directors, whether male or female, whatever be their experience or competence level in the ministry. I hope, too, that those who are seeking spiritual direction or already are enjoying its wonderful fruits will find this work useful.

I believe without reservation that the Kingdom of God is about relationships. In his word and work, his life and death, Jesus tried to show us how we could be with one another. In essence, spiritual direction is an act of Kingdom-making, for it empowers both director and directee to be loving and forgiving, as are Jesus and his God.

Men and women act with God in co-creating their lives by the decisions that they make. Spiritual direction is often a decisive method in discerning decisions that lead peacefully to the living God. If for no other reason, spiritual direction is and will remain among the more important ministries for the Christian community. *Guided by the Spirit* can certainly help directors and directees in discerning such life-shaping decisions. This is its purpose. This is its aim. This is its value.

Bibliography

Barry, William A., S.J. *Spiritual Direction and the Encounter with God: A Theological Inquiry.* Mahwah, N.J.: Paulist Press, 1992.

Barry, William A., S.J., and William Connolly S.J. *The Practice of Spiritual Direction.* New York: Seabury Press, 1982.

Cranmer, Leonard. *Up from Depression.* New York: Simon and Schuster, 1969.

Dyckman, Katherine Marie, S.N.J.M., and L. Patrick Carroll, S.J. *Inviting the Mystic, Supporting the Prophet.* Mahwah, N.J.: Paulist Press, 1981.

Fischer, Kathleen. *Women at the Well.* Mahwah, N.J.: Paulist Press, 1988.

Fleming, David L., S.J. *The Spiritual Exercises of St. Ignatius: A Literal Translation and a Contemporary Reading.* St. Louis, Mo.: Institute of Jesuit Sources, 1978.

Futrell, John, S.J. "Ignatian Discernment." *Studies in the Spirituality of Jesuits* 2, no. 2 (February 1970).

Gelpi, Donald, S.J. "The Converting Jesuit." *Studies in the Spirituality of Jesuits* 18, no. 1 (January 1986).

Green, Thomas H., S.J. *When the Well Runs Dry.* Notre Dame, Ind.: Ave Maria Press, 1979.

———. *Weeds Among the Wheat.* Notre Dame, Ind.: Ave Maria Press, 1984.

————. *Drinking from a Dry Well.* Notre Dame, Ind.: Ave Maria Press, 1991.

Hart, Thomas. *The Art of Christian Listening.* Mahwah, N.J.: Paulist Press, 1980.

Hassel, David J., S.J. *Radical Prayer.* Mahwah, N.J.: Paulist Press, 1983.

Larkin, Ernest, O. Carm. *Silent Presence.* Denville, N.J.: Dimension Books, 1981.

Lonergan, Bernard, S.J. "Dimensions of Meaning." In *Collection.* New York: Herder and Herder, 1967.

Page, Rose, O.C.D. "Direction in the Various Stages of Spiritual Development." *Contemplative Review* 12 (fall 1979): 11–18.

Purvis, Sally B. "Christian Feminist Spirituality." In *World Spirituality.* Vol. 18. Edited by Louis Dupre and Don E. Saliers. New York: Crossroad, 1989.

Rambo, Lewis R. *Understanding Religious Conversion.* New Haven, Conn.: Yale University Press, 1993.

Rogers, Carl. "Client-Centered Psychotherapy." In *Comprehensive Textbook of Psychiatry II.* 2nd ed. Edited by Alfred M. Freeman, Harold Kaplan, and Benjamin J. Saddock. New York: Williams and Wilkins, 1975.

Schneiders, Sandra, I.H.M. "The Contemporary Ministry of Spiritual Direction." *Chicago Studies* 15 (spring 1976): 119–35.

Toner, Jules, S.J. *A Commentary on St. Ignatius' Rules for the Discernment of Spirits.* St. Louis, Mo.: Institute of Jesuit Sources, 1982.

———. *Discerning God's Will.* St. Louis, Mo.: Institute of Jesuit Sources, 1991.

Ulanov, Ann, and Barry Ulanov. *Primary Speech.* Atlanta: John Knox Press, 1982.

Index